Personal, biblical, creative, experiential, powerful. Sharing from his heart, Drew Dickens takes the Bible and uses his creativity to lead you into powerfully experiencing God's presence.

Dr. Ronnie W. Floyd, speaker, author, ministry strategist, and pastor emeritus of Cross Church

May God bless this unique devotional, which will encourage and equip Christians to glorify the Lord's wonderful name.

Ray Comfort, founder and CEO of Living Waters, best-selling author, and cohost of the award-winning television program *Way of the Master*

Whispers of the Spirit is a beautiful book and will lift your heart to a higher place as you learn to listen to God's gentle voice in all things.

Marie Chapian, author of *Quiet Prayer: 31 Days of Meditation for Women* and host of the *Quiet Prayer Christian Meditation* podcast

Drew Dickens shares and shows that biblical meditation is neither magical nor mystical, neither shamanistic nor contentless. It is a sacred mystery, deliberately anchored in Scripture and personally applicable. Thus, it engages one's heart and mind via the bridge of the soul for spiritual strength. Learn to practice listening for the still, small voice in an intimate relationship with the living and loving God.

Dr. Ramesh Richard, theologian-evangelist, philosopher-expositor, and educator-author

I have known Drew for over thirty years, and his insights, care, and approach bring a much-appreciated calm as he inspires tens of thousands through his daily podcast. With this forty-day devotional, Drew poignantly captures one of my favorite Bible stories: Elijah searching for God through prayer and finding him in a profound way.

Whispers of the Spirit is a helpful tool for anyone longing to hear the whispers of the Spirit through a focused, intimate prayer life.

David Pierce, chief media officer of K-Love Radio Networks

Having heard Drew speak and seen him teach, lead, and guide others on the spiritual areas covered in *Whispers of the Spirit*, let me encourage you to engage and participate. Drew's unique and passionate relationship with Jesus Christ and ever-deepening faith encourage us all.

Rt. Rev. Philip Jones, senior pastor of All Saints Dallas and lead bishop of Anglican Mission in America

Even for busy people, perhaps particularly for busy people, it is easier to find the time to be still than to use it well. Drew's guided meditations in *Whispers of the Spirit* will lead you to more fruitfully fill the time you find with God.

Dr. Robert Hunt, professor of Christian mission and interreligious relations and director of Global Theological Education at the Southern Methodist University Perkins School of Theology

Whispers of the Spirit will help strengthen your faith and increase your intimacy with God. The daily readings compiled by author Drew Dickens invite you to be still and find comfort and solace in hearing the voice of the Lord. These quiet moments soon have you entering sweet union and communion with our Creator, forcing you to hit the pause button, turn off the world, and tune in to the Lord. Take the journey. It will revolutionize your prayer life, help you develop healthy rhythms, and escape the dreaded road to burnout.

David Jones, executive director of the Palau Foundation for World Evangelism

Whispers of the Spirit

A 40-DAY GUIDE TO INTIMATE PRAYER

DR. DREW DICKENS

BroadStreet
PUBLISHING

BroadStreet Publishing® Group, LLC
Savage, Minnesota, USA
BroadStreetPublishing.com

Whispers of the Spirit: A 40-Day Guide to Intimate Prayer

9781424568970 (hardcover)
9781424568987 (ebook)

Cover and interior by Garborg Design Works | garborgdesign.com

Printed in China

25 26 27 28 29 5 4 3 2 1

If you've tuned in to many episodes of my *EncounterPodcast*, then you know I proudly bear the title of grandfather—one of my most cherished honors. Yet, as I penned the pages of this devotional, the Lord called our youngest grandson, William, to his heavenly embrace. He was only eighteen months old, yet the concept of "too soon" was unknown to William. Innocence shielded him; all he recognized was each day's enveloping love. He lived day by day knowing he always was cherished, known, and nurtured, surrounded by nothing but the boundless affection of his family and friends. His absence is a silent ache within us all, yet through the words of this devotional, I hope to offer a tribute to William from his Pop, who misses him deeply.

*Heavenly Father, hear the groanings of my heart
and whispers of my spirit.*

*I beseech you to cradle my grandson William
in your loving arms.
Bathe him in love even deeper than he knew here among us.*

*Care for him, smile upon him,
and grant him peace.*

*And perhaps, in your heavenly kindness,
provide him a ball to play with. He would love that.*

In Jesus' name. Amen.

CONTENTS

Introduction

In the hush of Mount Horeb, Elijah found God not in the earthquake or fire but in a gentle whisper. This penetrating encounter mirrors the essence of the devotional journey you are about to enter. Here, in these pages, we will seek a sacred echo of the whisper Elijah encountered—a soft yet clear voice and divine presence guiding us through the bustling noise of our daily lives. Just as Elijah stood at the cave's entrance and awaited the whisper of God, so, too, are you and I invited to pause and find solace in the still, small voice of calm.

The intentional crafting of this devotional will draw you closer to God, allowing each whisper to transform the cacophony of life into a harmonious symphony with the Divine, where each quiet moment becomes a deep, personal communion with our Creator.

Over forty days, you and I will learn to rest in his loving presence, growing through many of the lost traditions and customs of the first-century church—ancient practices of guided meditative prayer, imaginative contemplation, and soulful breathing.

We embark on a unique journey to draw closer to our heavenly Friend. In these whispered moments, we discover God's voice speaking directly to our hearts, inviting us to rejoice in his eternal presence.

Through the whispers within this unique journey, you will not merely read words but engage in a divine dialogue that will transform your soul. Embrace this transformative journey, and you will emerge with a faith deeply rooted in the power of God's whispers.

Silence

Beginning a Journey to a Quiet Time

> "Be still, and know that I am God."
> PSALM 46:10

In the stillness, whirlwinds in your mind too often bring agitation, yet the divine whisper of Psalm 46 still beckons you to a sacred halt: "Be still, and know that I am God." This command invites you into a transformative journey that begins not with steps but with stillness.

In the quiet, tranquility is countercultural to a world that prizes noise. Yet it is in this holy pause that we truly encounter God. As you quiet your heart, you allow his voice to rise above the noise of your daily life. God often speaks through the quiet reassurance of his presence when we step away from the chaos and listen for him.

In this sacred moment, as you embark on this still, quiet journey, may you discover the rich depths of knowing God more intimately. Let the stillness be your sanctuary, where you encounter the Divine in the most personal and transformative ways. For in the quiet, the divine presence becomes apparent, the holy guidance more evident, and heavenly love more deeply felt from the Father, Son, and Holy Spirit.

GUIDED MEDITATION

Focused Scriptural Meditation

Quiet your heart before the Lord and reflect on Psalm 46:10. Hear his gentle whisper: *Be still, and know that I am God.* Acknowledge his majesty over all creation.

Reflective Prayer and Listening

Feel the burdens of your heart lighten as you recognize God's sovereignty. Know he is your ever-present help in times of trouble.

Contemplation and Gratitude

Rest in the assurance of God's unchanging nature. In gratitude, experience the peace that comes from knowing him.

IMAGINATIVE CONTEMPLATION

Contemplation of Psalm 46 begins like a leaf floating on a tranquil pond. We must pause to listen for the divine whisper to be still and know in the hush of nature's clasp.

Imagine yourself in a serene landscape, nestled beneath the vast canvas of a shimmering night sky. A gentle breeze guides a leaf over the smooth surface of the water.

You can't help but feel the presence of the Almighty holding you. Each breath becomes a silent prayer, surrendering to his sovereignty and your place within his creation. In this sacred moment, the worries of life dissolve, and a clear understanding emerges—God is in control, a steadfast protector and guide. The experience leaves you with a quiet faith and a peaceful spirit.

ECHOED VERSES

Hold (hands over heart):

I am still and know that you are my heavenly Father.

Receive (hands open):

Lord, in stillness, your presence calms my restless heart.

Hold (hands over heart):

You, Lord Christ, will be exalted among the nations.

Receive (hands open):

You are exalted in my life, and your majesty fills every moment.

Hold (hands over heart):

Holy Spirit, you will be exalted on the earth.

Receive (hands open):

In your creation, your glory resonates around and within me.

SOULFUL BREATHING

Let your body relax, hands resting gently by your side or in your lap. Close your eyes and take a slow, deep breath through your nose. Feel the air filling your lungs and hold it gently. As you inhale, silently say in your heart, *Help me be still.*

Slowly exhale through your mouth and internally recite, *I know that you are God.* Continue this pattern for several moments.

Inhale: *Help me be still.*

Exhale: *I know that you are God.*

Remain in silence, basking in the peace and presence of God. Then conclude with gratitude by gently opening your eyes and whispering a prayer of thanks to God for his ever-present help and assurance in your life.

SOULFUL REFLECTIONS

As you embrace the stillness, what subtle messages or feelings do you sense from God, and how do they speak to your current life situation?

Reflect on the moments of silence you experienced today. How did they shift your perspective or feelings about your daily life and relationship with God?

CLOSING BENEDICTION

May you discover stillness in the Lord's everlasting presence, a sanctuary of peace in the turbulence of life. As the timeless words of Psalm 46 gently whisper into your being, "Be still, and know that I am God," let this divine assurance resonate within your heart. In this sacred stillness, may you find a respite for your soul, a moment to breathe in the majesty and grace of our Creator. Amid life's fiercest storms and unrelenting chaos, may you recognize his sovereign hand guiding you, feel the gentle touch of his calming grace, and be enveloped in the comforting truth of his unchanging love. As you step through your day, may you carry this sacred stillness within you, a testament to his enduring love and strength. Now go in peace, knowing God is your refuge and strength in every moment of every day. In Jesus' name. Amen.

Basics

Learning to Communicate Godward

Do not be anxious about anything, but in every situation, by prayer
and petition, with thanksgiving, present your requests to God.
PHILIPPIANS 4:6 NIV

In the stillness, when your heart yearns for a refuge, Philippians 4
whispers a divine invitation: "Present your requests to God." Here lies
the essence of prayer, an open-hearted conversation with God, where
your worries, gratitude, and desires intertwine in a sacred trust.

In the quiet, prayer becomes more than a ritual. It's an intimate
journey through which your soul finds its authentic voice. You can
release your anxieties in the landscape of worship. Here you lay down
your troubles at the feet of the Almighty not as an act of defeat but as
a surrender, a powerful declaration of your dependence on God.

In this sacred moment, your heart swells with gratitude.
Thanksgiving is the melody that harmonizes your requests, reminding
you of God's past faithfulness and his unchanging nature. In this
symphony of supplication and thanks, you find peace that transcends
understanding guarding your heart and mind in Christ Jesus. Your
prayers become a sanctuary, inviting you to bring everything before
the heavenly Father, Son, and Holy Spirit.

GUIDED MEDITATION

Focused Scriptural Meditation

Let the words of Philippians 4:6 guide your heart and mind. Embrace this moment of tranquility, knowing that in the presence of the Divine, your worries transform into peace.

Reflective Prayer and Listening

Pray this passage, allowing it to permeate your being. Share your thoughts and feelings with God and listen for his gentle response.

Contemplation and Gratitude

Rest in this peace, feeling gratitude for God's presence. Carry this serenity into your day, letting it be a beacon of his love.

IMAGINATIVE CONTEMPLATION

Imagine a tranquil garden bathed in dawn's soft, golden light. Here, in the symphony of creation, your heart unburdens its worries onto the path of prayer. See this path stretching out before you—smooth, level, and even.

Each step you take is a whispered petition, a plea wrapped in gratitude, floating upward like the morning mist on a dove's wing. With your eyes closed, open your mind's eye to see the Holy Spirit encasing you with the promise of the divine presence, enveloping you in a peace that transcends all understanding. In this sacred space, lay your worries down on level ground at the foot of the cross.

ECHOED VERSES

Hold (hands over heart):

>*Heavenly Father, you calm my anxious thoughts.*

Receive (hands open):

>*I claim your peace, which surpasses understanding.*

Hold (hands over heart):

>*Jesus, you hear every heartfelt prayer.*

Receive (hands open):

>*In gratitude, I receive your answers.*

Hold (hands over heart):

>*Holy Spirit, guide my every petition.*

Receive (hands open):

>*Your wisdom flows into my life.*

SOULFUL BREATHING

Allow your eyes to drift into a gentle gaze. As you breathe deeply, let your eyelids grow heavy and gradually close without effort. As your eyes eventually softly shut, turn your focus inward to the sacred space within your heart. Gently and deeply inhale, envisioning the breath as God's calming presence entering you. As you inhale, silently affirm, *Lord, I place my worries in you.* Feel his grace filling your lungs, your heart, your very being. Hold it.

Now exhale slowly, releasing your anxieties and fears to him. As you exhale, whisper within, *Your peace surpasses all understanding.* Visualize your worries drifting away, dissolved by his loving presence.

Inhale: *Lord, I place my worries in you.*

Exhale: *Your peace surpasses all understanding.*

Repeat this breathing cycle several times. With each inhale, draw in trust and surrender; with each release, cast off anxiety and cling to peace. In this sacred rhythm, find your heart aligning with his eternal promise of peace and care.

SOULFUL REFLECTIONS

As you welcome the stillness, in what ways are you encountering God's presence in both your moments of joy and your times of challenge?

How might being thankful in all circumstances draw you closer to the heart of God and enhance your understanding of his love and purpose for you?

CLOSING BENEDICTION

May you enter God's sanctuary with an open heart, knowing you are heard, loved, and held in the presence of the Father, Son, and Holy Spirit. Feel your anxieties dissolve into the hands of the Almighty as he reminds you that in every moment, his grace, love, and mercy are sufficient. May the peace of the Lord, which surpasses all understanding, guard your heart and mind. As you step forward into the world, may you remember not to be anxious about anything. In every situation, through prayer and petition with thanksgiving, present your requests to God. May his presence be your constant companion, guiding you in every decision and calming every fear. Let gratitude fill your heart and trust in his unfailing love and provision. Now go forth in the assurance of his peace, always embracing each day with faith and courage. In Jesus' name. Amen.

Routine

Creating Consistent Prayer Habits

Pray without ceasing.
1 THESSALONIANS 5:17

In the stillness, the quiet call of God whispers through the racket and invites you into a calm space. There you find the gentle whisper of Scripture urging you toward a ceaseless communion with the Divine. "Pray without ceasing," a simple yet heartfelt decree, calls you not to a task of relentless chattering but to a continuous spiritual connection. It's an invitation to weave prayer into the very fabric of your daily life, transforming ordinary moments into sacred encounters.

In the quiet, as you cultivate this habit of ceaseless prayer, you will learn to listen to the subtle movements of the Spirit guiding and comforting you. This practice of persistent prayer is not about the frequency of your words but about the consistency of your attention to God.

In this sacred moment, may this day be a gentle journey into the heart of prayer, where you find a routine and a rhythm of living in constant awareness of God's abiding presence. Let your life become a prayer, a living testament to the peace and serenity of the unceasing embrace of the Father, Son, and Holy Spirit.

GUIDED MEDITATION

Focused Scriptural Meditation

Read 1 Thessalonians 5:17 and feel the presence of God surrounding you, his light filling you with peace.

Reflective Prayer and Listening

Sense the gentle nudge of the Holy Spirit. Each beat of your heart becomes an unspoken prayer.

Contemplation and Gratitude

Rest in this sacred space and be thankful and fully aware that in every moment, you are in the loving arms of your Creator.

IMAGINATIVE CONTEMPLATION

Imagine yourself in a humble dwelling in Thessalonica in the peaceful tranquility of an early morning. Soft light filters through the window, casting a warm glow on the weathered parchment of Paul's letter. As you unroll the scroll, the words from 1 Thessalonians 5 come alive, whispering truths into the stillness.

Envision the early believers gathered closely, absorbing Paul's counsel to encourage and be patient. Feel the unity and love in their midst, the gentle strength of their faith.

Reflect on the penetrating impact of this message in your own life. Allow the scene to deepen your understanding of what it means to live with ceaseless prayer, joy, and gratitude. Feel a thorough connection with the Divine and a timeless link between the early Christians and your spiritual journey in this contemplative moment.

ECHOED VERSES

Hold (hands over heart):

Heavenly Father, you call me to rejoice always in your love.

Receive (hands open):

In joy, I welcome your love, which fills my heart with peace.

Hold (hands over heart):

Lord Christ, you teach me to pray continually.

Receive (hands open):

In prayer, I find strength and constant communion with you.

Hold (hands over heart):

Holy Spirit, you urge me to give thanks in all circumstances.

Receive (hands open):

In gratitude, I see your hand in every aspect of my life.

SOULFUL BREATHING

Breathe deeply, drawing in peace and exhaling any tension. As you breathe in, envision God's presence filling you with his unending love.

With each exhale, release all your worries, surrendering them to his care.

Inhale: *Pray continually.*

Exhale: *Without ceasing.*

As you continue, let your breaths become a silent prayer, a call to an ever-present dialogue with God. Let this rhythmic breathing remind you of your constant connection with the Divine. Conclude with a moment of gratitude, cherishing the peace that comes from this sacred communion. Rest in this stillness, allowing 1 Thessalonians 5:17's message of ceaseless prayer to resonate within your heart, strengthening your bond with the Lord.

SOULFUL REFLECTIONS

How does continual prayer shape your daily life and deepen your relationship with God?

In moments of silence, what insights about God's presence and guidance do you discover in the stillness of your heart?

CLOSING BENEDICTION

Now release your worries and distractions, aligning your heart with God through constant prayer and guiding your thoughts toward unceasing conversation with the Lord while wrapped in his peace and care. May you rest here in a silent yet powerful connection with the Divine and feel the weight of his guidance. May you sense manifest hope as Paul's words urge you to constantly rejoice, pray, and give thanks in all circumstances. May the Lord bless you and keep you in unceasing prayer. As you journey through each day, may your heart always be attuned to God's gentle whispers guiding and comforting you. May the Holy Spirit inspire your every word and thought, turning them into a ceaseless offering of love and praise to your heavenly Father. In your moments of stillness and hours of busyness, may you feel the steadfast presence of God enfolding you in his grace and peace. Now, in the name of Jesus Christ, go forth in the assurance of his love and presence. Amen.

Engage

Deepening Word-Centered Meditation

"This Book of the Law shall not depart from your mouth,
but you shall meditate on it day and night."
JOSHUA 1:8

In the stillness of your heart, there is a place unmarred by the relentless roar of life's demands, a sanctuary where the soul can bask in a holy pause. Here is an invitation to a deeper communion, a call to embed God's words not just in your mind but in the fabric of your existence. A call to engage.

In the quiet, as you meditate without ceasing, the words of Scripture fill your lungs, circulate through your veins, and settle in your heart. This is the essence of Word-centered meditation, a time for allowing God's living, breathing Word to engage your soul.

In the sacred, you encounter the divine mysteries, where the lines between the heavenly and the earthly blur, and you touch the hem of eternity. Let his words remind you that you are never alone in the depths of stillness, for he speaks life into your being. He is there, desiring to engage with you, his child, a child of the Father, Son, and Holy Spirit.

GUIDED MEDITATION

Focused Scriptural Meditation

As you reflect on Joshua 1:8, feel your heart open to its wisdom.
Visualize God's words as a guiding light within, illuminating your path.

Reflective Prayer and Listening

In conversation with God, let go of distractions, centering your
thoughts on his teachings and walking in serene harmony with his will.

Contemplation and Gratitude

Accept the tranquility with thanksgiving, letting his wisdom resonate.
His presence beckons you, and you are grounded in his truth.

IMAGINATIVE CONTEMPLATION

In the twilight of Canaan, at the threshold of the promised land, your
feet stand in the shallows of the Jordan River. It swirls with hope and
promise that beckon you forward.

Feel the weight of Moses' mantle resting upon your shoulders. It's
a cloak woven from obedience, heavy with the legacy of a journey
through the wilderness. As you gaze across the river, you can almost
hear God's voice calling you to enter the unknown.

In this moment, the river becomes more than a barrier; it
symbolizes transformation, a crossing over from past to future, from
doubt to belief. You realize that with every step you take in faith, you
are drawing closer not only to the land of promise but also to the
heart of God.

ECHOED VERSES

Hold (hands over heart):

Heavenly Father, guide me with your eternal wisdom and love.

Receive (hands open):

I open my heart to your guiding light within me.

Hold (hands over heart):

Lord Christ, I find strength and unyielding courage in your words.

Receive (hands open):

Your strength fills me, empowering my every step forward.

Hold (hands over heart):

Holy Spirit, your teachings anchor me during my life's storms.

Receive (hands open):

I receive your peace, which secures my soul in tranquility.

SOULFUL BREATHING

Take a deep, calming breath, filling your lungs with stillness and peace. With each inhale, draw in the wisdom and presence of God, letting his words fill you. Hold this breath so they may not depart from you.

As you exhale slowly, release any tension or distraction of the day. Feel your connection to God's teachings deepen as his wisdom permeates your being.

Inhale: *I keep your Word close.*

Exhale: *I meditate on it day and night.*

Conclude with a moment of gratitude for this time of reflection. Allow the stillness and Joshua 1:8's message to resonate in your heart and mind, fostering a more insightful sense of inner peace and divine connection.

SOULFUL REFLECTIONS

In what ways does meditating on God's law, as urged in Joshua 1:8, shape your daily actions and decisions, drawing you closer to the Lord's heart?

How does the commitment not to let Scripture depart from your mouth impact your conversations and how you express yourself to others?

CLOSING BENEDICTION

May the whispers of divine truth echo in this sacred closing benediction as you breathe in the Word of God. May Scripture shape your thoughts, guide your actions, and engage your soul. Let his words remind you that you are never alone in the depths of stillness, for God speaks life into your being. He is there, desiring to engage with you, his child. May the love of the Father fill you, the grace of Jesus nurture you, and the fellowship of the Holy Spirit guide your path. As you walk in obedience, let your life be a ceaseless prayer. May God's wisdom illuminate your journey, his peace calm your soul, and his strength uphold you in every trial. Go forth in the assurance of his love, knowing that he is with you today and always. In the name of Jesus. Amen.

Gratitude

Thanking God Daily

Give thanks in all circumstances;
for this is the will of God in Christ Jesus for you.
1 THESSALONIANS 5:18

In the stillness of your heart, it is possible to become ungrateful, yet there is that gentle, divine nudge toward a sacred rhythm of gratitude. In these quiet moments away from the chaos, you can find the space to acknowledge the endless gifts God has bestowed upon you. In daily thanksgiving, your heart aligns with the heart of God, transforming your perspective and turning even the mundane into a holy encounter.

In the silence, as you reflect on your day, notice how the subtle threads of grace weave through even the most ordinary moments. The warmth of the sun, the smile of a stranger, the comfort of a familiar scent—each is a brushstroke of God's love. This daily gratitude ritual is not about dismissing your challenges but about finding God's presence within them as your spirit soars, connecting you to the eternal.

In the sacred, consider this day a deliberate break from the relentless pursuit of doing. In every circumstance, gratitude anchors you to the unchanging love of the Father, Son, and Holy Spirit.

GUIDED MEDITATION

Focused Scriptural Meditation
As you read 1 Thessalonians 5:18, picture your heart aligning with God's rhythm. Reflect on the blessings of the beauty of creation and the gift of life.

Reflective Prayer and Listening
In your soul's quiet sanctuary, offer a prayer of thanks for all you have, are, and will be.

Contemplation and Gratitude
Embrace a sense of peace and gratitude. Know that God is with you in every moment, guiding and loving you.

IMAGINATIVE CONTEMPLATION

Envision yourself in Thessalonica, in northeastern Greece, at the northern end of the Thermaic Gulf. You stand in a simple room aglow with the light of flickering candles. Paul's words from his letter echo through the gathering of early believers.

As the words "Rejoice always, pray without ceasing, give thanks in all circumstances" (vv. 16–18) fill the space, a truth settles in your soul. You feel the weight of your daily struggles, yet a divine lightness settles within you, a divine tension.

At this moment, the presence of God is tangible; your heart swells with gratitude, and you realize that God is whispering an invitation to a life of ceaseless prayer and boundless joy.

ECHOED VERSES

Hold (hands over heart):

Heavenly Father, guide me through every season with love.

Receive (hands open):

In your guidance, I find peace and unwavering faith.

Hold (hands over heart):

Lord Christ, I see unending grace and mercy in your sacrifice.

Receive (hands open):

Through your grace, my spirit is renewed and strengthened.

Hold (hands over heart):

Holy Spirit, your presence fills me with life-changing thankfulness.

Receive (hands open):

As I embrace your presence, my heart overflows with joy and gratitude.

SOULFUL BREATHING

Take a deep breath, filling your lungs with peace and stillness. As you inhale, receive gratitude, feeling it permeate your being. Hold this breath for a moment, contemplating the countless blessings in your life.

Now exhale slowly, releasing any burdens or worries. With each exhale, reflect on the wisdom of giving thanks in all circumstances, understanding that God is with you in every moment.

Inhale: *In everything, give thanks.*

Exhale: *For this is God's will.*

Continue this pattern of inhaling gratitude, exhaling trust. Let these breaths become a rhythm, a prayer of thankfulness. Sit in stillness, renewed and connected, with a sense of peace and gratitude.

SOULFUL REFLECTIONS

In what ways have you experienced God's presence in both your moments of joy and your times of challenge?

How might being thankful draw you closer to the heart of God and enhance your understanding of his love and purpose for you?

CLOSING BENEDICTION

In this space where heaven touches earth, may you recognize God's constant presence in every aspect of your life. Carry this peace and gratitude forward, allowing it to infuse every part of your day. Here, in this holy stillness, may you grasp that gratitude is not just an act but a constant acknowledgment of God's unwavering faithfulness. As you cultivate this heart of thanksgiving, let it not be confined to moments of abundance but also shine as a beacon of hope in times of scarcity. May the peace of the Lord Christ go with you. May God give you words of thanks in all circumstances, for this is his will in Christ Jesus for you. May he lead you when you are lost and keep you safe from harm. May he make you happy with all the amazing things you see as he brings you back home in the name of Jesus. Amen.

Confession

Acknowledging Sins Openly

If we confess our sins, he is faithful and just to forgive us our sins
and to cleanse us from all unrighteousness.

1 JOHN 1:9

In the stillness, listen for a whisper that guides you toward the light of confession. The world around you buzzes with ceaseless activity, the whirlwind of life's demands often drowning out the soft voice of the Spirit. Yet you find a haven in this space of quiet reflection.

In the silence, invite yourself to lay bare the truths of your heart, to unveil the sins that weigh heavily on your spirit—not in judgment but in liberation. As you openly acknowledge your transgressions before God, a divine exchange occurs. The lightness of his grace lifts the burden of your sins, replacing it with divine serenity.

In this sacred moment of introspection, remember that the journey of faith is not about achieving perfection but about embracing continual renewal. Each act of confession is a step toward deeper fellowship with God. Acknowledge the importance of this practice as you realize God forgives, loves, and restores you and let your heart overflow with the peace of the Father, Son, and Holy Spirit.

GUIDED MEDITATION

Focused Scriptural Meditation

Reflect on Psalm 55 as you acknowledge the burdens of sins and regrets in your heart.

Reflective Prayer and Listening

Release these burdens as if you were casting them into a clear stream and watching them float away.

Contemplation and Gratitude

Rest in the knowledge that God has forgiven you and cherishes you. Let the peace of God wash over you. Receive this freedom and renewal with gratitude.

IMAGINATIVE CONTEMPLATION

Imagine yourself in the morning twilight when the first light of dawn has not yet touched the earth. You are not alone; beside you is the apostle John, his eyes alight with a wisdom born of deep communion with God.

As he talks, it's as if his words of forgiveness bring to life the essence of God's presence. Every word is a light that represents the truth of God's love, a love that illuminates even the darkest corners of your soul.

You understand that each confession and act of forgiveness transforms you from within. As you give and receive mercy, your soul journeys toward a more intimate relationship with God. This contemplative experience leaves you with a sense of peace, a reminder that you will always find hope, renewal, and forgiveness in God's loving presence.

ECHOED VERSES

Hold (hands over heart):

Heavenly Father, your mercy removes my every failure and sin.

Receive (hands open):

I accept your forgiveness and allow it to wash me clean and new.

Hold (hands over heart):

Lord Christ, in your love, you transform my guilt into grace.

Receive (hands open):

Gratefully, I receive your grace, feeling peace and freedom.

Hold (hands over heart):

Holy Spirit, your presence guides me to truth and light.

Receive (hands open):

I open my heart to your guidance, feeling enlightened and loved.

SOULFUL BREATHING

Breathe and fill your lungs with God's endless mercy. As you inhale, silently acknowledge your need for his forgiveness. Hold this breath gently, feeling his love surrounding you.

Now exhale slowly, releasing your sins and mistakes into his care. Feel the weight of your transgressions lifting.

Inhale: *You are faithful and just.*

Exhale: *Forgive me and cleanse me of my sin.*

As you engage in this breathing cycle, accept the grace to rest deeply in it, inviting the unwavering truth of his promise to settle gently into your heart. Conclude this sacred time with a moment of stillness, embracing the abiding peace God generously fills you with, a testament to his everlasting love and faithfulness.

SOULFUL REFLECTIONS

In what ways have you experienced God's faithful forgiveness in your life, and how have those encounters transformed your understanding of his grace and love for you?

Reflect on the moments when you have held back from confessing your sins to God. What fears or beliefs hindered this openness?

CLOSING BENEDICTION

Amid this tranquility, may the words of 1 John 1 resonate with clarity that guides you back to the path of righteousness. By the grace of God through faith in Christ, may you know the cleansing flood of forgiveness that leaves behind a purity that only his love can bestow, a testament to his unfailing kindness and justice. May the Lord bless you with the courage to confess your sins, knowing that in his boundless mercy, he is faithful and will forgive. As you walk in the freedom of his forgiveness, may your heart be filled with peace and your spirit renewed by his love. Now may you find strength in your vulnerability and confessions and discover the transformative depths of his unfailing love. Go forth in the assurance of his grace, carrying the joy of redemption in your heart. In Jesus' name. Amen.

Guidance

Requesting God's Direction

If any of you lacks wisdom, let him ask God,
who gives generously to all without reproach,
and it will be given him.
JAMES 1:5

In the stillness, you find a whisper more potent than the world's roar around you. In these moments, when the hustle of life fades into the background, your heart can truly listen. The stillness is pure and untouched, allowing God's guidance to flow into your soul without forcing it. The world urges you to rush, but true wisdom awaits those who pause to listen.

In the quiet, your spirit learns the language of the heavens. Away from life's demands, you discover that silence is not an absence but a presence. Each quiet moment is a step closer to the heart of God, where the complexities of life meet the simplicity of eternal truth.

In the sacred presence of God, the soul delicately blossoms and opens. Here the inward journey encounters the Divine where the whispers of God resonate within you. Heavenly wisdom is not just a concept but a presence that leads you ever closer to the truth and light of the Father, Son, and Holy Spirit.

GUIDED MEDITATION

Focused Scriptural Meditation

Embrace James 1:5 and the peace of God's presence. Allow the Holy Spirit to remind you that understanding is yours for the asking.

Reflective Prayer and Listening

With each breath, pray that you will draw closer to God, who is ready to provide wisdom generously without judgment, as you journey toward understanding.

Contemplation and Gratitude

Carry this tranquility and the assurance that divine wisdom will illuminate your path. Hold on to the confidence and gratitude you gain, letting it guide you.

IMAGINATIVE CONTEMPLATION

Envision yourself on a boat in a storm, waves crashing around you. The sky above mirrors your turmoil, echoing your trials. As the sea rages, you feel the surge of doubt and tribulations.

Yet in this chaos, there's a presence of peace. You sense a gentle whisper, more robust than the fiercest wind, calling you to steadfastness. It's as if God's hand were reaching out through the storm, offering himself as the anchor.

The scene transforms your understanding of trials. They are not merely obstacles but divine invitations to receive wisdom and grow closer to God. This contemplation leaves you with renewed courage and an unshakable trust in the divine guidance that navigates you through life's stormiest seas.

ECHOED VERSES

Hold (hands over heart):

Father God, you know my heart, my need for wisdom.

Receive (hands open):

I open myself to your divine guidance and truth.

Hold (hands over heart):

Lord Christ, I trust you for understanding in trials.

Receive (hands open):

I receive your strength, embracing each challenge with faith.

Hold (hands over heart):

Holy Spirit, your wisdom is a light in my darkness.

Receive (hands open):

I welcome your light, which illuminates my path with clarity.

SOULFUL BREATHING

Take a deep, slow breath, filling your lungs with peace and stillness. As you inhale, think, *Lord, I ask for wisdom.* Feel the generosity of God's Spirit entering your being.

Now exhale slowly, envisioning any doubt or confusion leaving your body. Feel yourself receiving the gift of divine understanding.

Inhale: *Lord, I ask for wisdom.*

Exhale: *And your wisdom flows.*

As you breathe, allow Scripture to settle gently into the depths of your heart. Feel a deep and penetrating connection with God. Allow each breath to remind you that his wisdom is perpetually within reach and be comforted by that knowledge. Your breathing is a divine meeting place where his eternal truths resonate within you, offering guidance and peace.

SOULFUL REFLECTIONS

In moments of uncertainty and challenge, how do you actively seek God's wisdom, and how does this openness to his guidance transform your understanding and decisions?

Reflect on a time when you felt God's wisdom guiding you. How did this experience deepen your trust in his plan and change how you approach life's trials and decisions?

CLOSING BENEDICTION

Even though the tumultuous cover of dark, swirling clouds may shroud you, may you feel the assurance of God affirming your quest for wisdom and peace. May your day become a sacred space where the chatter of daily life does not drown out the soothing voice of God. May the Lord bless you with the wisdom that comes from above, pure and peaceful, resolute in wielding truth, not yielding to the turmoil of the world. May he fill your heart with understanding and guide your steps with his light. May the peace of God, which surpasses all understanding, guard your heart and mind in Christ Jesus. And in the journey ahead, may you always find his generous wisdom guiding you, lighting your path, and enriching your spirit. In the name of Jesus, go forth equipped and uplifted in the grace and knowledge of our Lord. Amen.

Listen

Hearing Divine Whispers

"My sheep hear my voice,
and I know them,
and they follow me."
JOHN 10:27

In the stillness, where the world's blaring fades into a whisper, you find a space for your soul to listen, an oasis untouched by the busyness of daily life. In this tranquil haven, the voice of God is not a thunderous roar but a soft, steady calling. Here you begin to hear the thought-provoking truths that often escape you amid the noise of everyday life.

In the quiet, your heart becomes receptive to God's divine wisdom and understanding. This silent sanctuary frees you from distractions that often cloud your spiritual vision. The quiet is not emptiness; it's a fullness of presence where God knows and cherishes every unspoken worry, every unformed thought. In these moments, his voice becomes clear, guiding you gently.

In the sacred, faith deepens, and the soul discovers its true north. Remember that you are not merely wandering through life; a purposeful, tender hand leads you. A voice transforms, guides, and reassures you. Such is the power of divine whispers from the Father, Son, and Holy Spirit.

GUIDED MEDITATION

Focused Scriptural Meditation

As you read John 10:27, feel God's presence. His voice is a comforting melody, calling you by name. You are known.

Reflective Prayer and Listening

As you commune with the Divine, acknowledge the assurance of his guidance. He is with you, leading you along a unique path.

Contemplation and Gratitude

Rest in the certainty of his love and guidance, clothing you in peace and thankfulness. Move forward with the assurance that you can intimately connect with God.

IMAGINATIVE CONTEMPLATION

Picture yourself standing in rolling hills of emerald grasses. Near you stands the Good Shepherd. His eyes scan the horizon. Each beloved creature grazes under his watchful gaze.

You are one of his sheep, cherished and known. The Shepherd calls out to you by name, his voice a soothing melody. You are supposed to answer his call. In this moment, the boundary between the divine and the earthly blurs, and you feel an overwhelming sense of belonging.

This is not just a scene of pastoral beauty; it's a perceptive revelation of being known, guided, and loved. As you contemplate this, let your heart accept that you are never alone in life's vast field. The Good Shepherd is always guiding, calling, and loving.

ECHOED VERSES

Hold (hands over heart):

Heavenly Father, you know me, and in your love, you hold me.

Receive (hands open):

I welcome your presence, feeling peace and intense love.

Hold (hands over heart):

Lord Christ, I find strength, purpose, and direction in your guidance.

Receive (hands open):

Open to your path, I walk in faith and trust.

Hold (hands over heart):

Holy Spirit, your presence calls me with a whisper of divine intimacy.

Receive (hands open):

Listening intently, I receive your wisdom, grace, and comfort.

SOULFUL BREATHING

As you inhale, silently say to yourself, *Your sheep hear your voice*, and feel the assurance of belonging. Draw in the comfort of being known by him, the Good Shepherd.

Exhale slowly, whispering in your heart, *I follow you*, as you release any tension or doubt. Surrender to his guidance. Each exhale is a release into his care. Feel the deepening of your connection to the Divine.

Inhale: *Your sheep hear your voice.*

Exhale: *I follow you.*

Conclude with a moment of stillness to allow these truths to resonate within you. In this quietness, know the calm and connection you have fostered with God. Carry this peace with you and remain grounded in his presence and protection.

SOULFUL REFLECTIONS

In moments of silence, how do you perceive God's voice guiding you, and how can you become more attuned to his gentle whisper in your daily life?

Reflect on the ways you have followed God's lead. How has this journey transformed your understanding of his love and purpose for you?

CLOSING BENEDICTION

May you feel the grasp of the hand that knows you more intimately than you know yourself, a hand that crafted you with divine precision and care. In every gentle breeze, may you hear the whispers of the Divine speaking directly to your heart. In the sacred stillness, may you find more than solace; find strength, peace, and your Creator's abiding love. May the Lord fill your heart with his understanding, guiding your steps in the light of his wisdom. In each trial, let his wisdom be your fortress, his Word your constant comfort. Let the peace of God, which surpasses all understanding, guard your heart and mind in Christ Jesus. As you move forward, may you sense his voice guiding you, his wisdom illuminating your path, and his love enriching your spirit. Go forth known and uplifted in the grace and knowledge of our Lord. Amen.

Requests

Sharing Personal Desires

Delight yourself in the Lord,
and he will give you the desires of your heart.
Psalm 37:4

In the stillness, where the world's hustle fades, you find a place of serenity. This verse whispers a timeless truth: in the tranquility of God's presence, your deepest desires and his eternal promises intertwine. Your wandering soul finds its way to align with his purpose.

In the quiet, your inner voice emerges uncluttered by the outer noise. Here you discover the essence of prayer; it's not a monologue but a dialogue with God. The quiet becomes a sanctuary where your words are less about making requests and more about receiving wisdom. Here God paints on your heart his desires, which resonate with his perfect plan for you.

In the sacred, where time seems to stand still, your spirit dances with his. This holy communion transcends words. In this sacred space, your desires meld with divine intention, and the whispers of your heart echo the voice of God. In this holy union, you find not just answers but also alignment and an overwhelming sense of belonging in the heart of the Father, Son, and Holy Spirit.

GUIDED MEDITATION

Focused Scriptural Meditation

As you read Psalm 37:4, notice your heart's deepest yearnings align with your Creator.

Reflective Prayer and Listening

In this time of heartfelt dialogue with God, visualize your desires as seeds watered by faith. See them flourishing under God's care.

Contemplation and Gratitude

With gratitude, rest in communion, knowing it brings you closer to God's heart, where true fulfillment comes from aligning your desires with the divine will.

IMAGINATIVE CONTEMPLATION

Envision a lush green field where the golden sun casts a warm, comforting glow. In the distance, a mighty tree stands tall, symbolizing steadfast faith.

Rest under its shade and plant yourself firmly in faith like this tree, drinking deeply from the waters of divine wisdom. Feel the quiet assurance that God nurtures and guides you as you commit your way to him, just as the sunlight and rain nourish the tree.

In this contemplative moment, the whispers of the wind echo a promise of peace and a future rooted in divine providence. Let this scene remind you to trust in the growth that the hands of God bring you. Feel your heart swell with an astute understanding of divine timing and care, drawing you closer to the heart of God.

ECHOED VERSES

Hold (hands over heart):

Heavenly Father, you are my heart's deepest desire.

Receive (hands open):

In your presence, my soul finds true joy.

Hold (hands over heart):

Lord Christ, I place my trust and hopes in you.

Receive (hands open):

Your love fulfills, surpassing my greatest dreams.

Hold (hands over heart):

Holy Spirit, you are my guiding light in the darkness.

Receive (hands open):

I receive your guidance and walk in your peace.

SOULFUL BREATHING

Inhale quietly, allowing your soul to absorb the abundant joy in God's hands. As you hold this breath, let your heart ponder the fullness of joy in his presence. It's a divine joy transcending worldly concerns, filling you with a serene assurance of his everlasting love and grace.

Now exhale slowly, releasing any worries or fears. Imagine letting go of what hinders your delight in him. Feel the tranquility that comes from trusting in his love.

Inhale: *Delight yourself in the Lord.*

Exhale: *And he will give.*

Continue this rhythmic breathing, allowing the message of this verse to resonate within you. With each breath, you feel more connected to God, more attuned to his voice.

SOULFUL REFLECTIONS

In what ways have you experienced your heart's desires aligning with God's will, and how has this shaped your understanding of true joy and fulfillment in him?

Reflect on the moments when you have felt distant from God's presence. What steps can you take to deepen your trust and find delight in him, even in times of uncertainty or challenge?

CLOSING BENEDICTION

In these tranquil interludes, so often fleeting amid life's roar, your spirit synchronizes with the divine cadence of creation. May the peace of God transcend all comprehension and stand guard over your heart and thoughts in Christ Jesus. As you step forward, may your desires align with his divine will, allowing you to discover your deepest fulfillment and contentment in him. Let the glow of his love light your path and his wisdom be your faithful guide. In moments of doubt and confusion's fog, may you find solace in his unfailing grace and become aware that true joy dwells in his presence. Go now encouraged and assured by his abiding love and shepherded by his Spirit. May you always lead a life that honors him. In all you do, reflect his glory in the precious name of Jesus. Amen.

Community

Strengthening Group Intercession

"Where two or three are gathered in my name,
there am I among them."
MATTHEW 18:20

In the stillness of your heart, there lies a sacred space for communion with the Almighty. As you step away from the clutter, you find yourself in a realm where each breath is a prayer, each moment a sanctuary. Here the words of Matthew remind you that in gatherings, even as small as two or three, the Lord's presence is tangible.

In the quiet of your soul, where the chaos of thoughts and fears subsides, there is a holy pause. The truth of God's Word blossoms in this calm, revealing its power and grace. This verse is an assurance of his presence and an invitation to experience the transformative mystery of communal prayer.

In the sacred assembly of believers, where hearts unite in intercession, you find a reflection of heaven itself. In this holy communion, you realize that prayer is not just a solitary venture but a symphony of souls. Each unique voice joins in a chorus of worship and supplication that ascends to the throne of the Father, Son, and Holy Spirit.

GUIDED MEDITATION

Focused Scriptural Meditation

Reflect on Matthew 18:20 and feel the unity and love of being encircled by fellow believers.

Reflective Prayer and Listening

Open your heart to this truth: in your unity, his Spirit thrives. Share your thoughts with God and listen for his comforting response.

Contemplation and Gratitude

Breathe in the reality of his constant presence. Offer thanks for your catalytic connection with God and others in faith.

IMAGINATIVE CONTEMPLATION

Imagine yourself in a room with walls that echo hushed prayers. Around you are faces of faith, eyes closed in devotion, hands clasped tightly.

In the center, you sense God's presence, a comforting warmth spreading through the room. Holy anticipation charges the atmosphere. In this gathering, Jesus is among you, unseen yet profoundly real.

His love binds all hearts together. You feel an overwhelming sense of belonging, of being known and understood. In this sacred communion, the burdens you carry seem lighter, as if lifted by unseen hands. The words of Christ resonate within you, a promise made real by his grace through the collective faith of those gathered around you and the depth of your own belief. This moment is a glimpse of the transcendent realm, a foretaste of eternal fellowship.

ECHOED VERSES

Hold (hands over heart):

Heavenly Father, I find you, my ever-present comfort, when I gather with believers.

Receive (hands open):

We welcome your comforting presence, Lord.

Hold (hands over heart):

Lord Christ, where hearts unite in your name, there you dwell abundantly.

Receive (hands open):

In unity, we feel your abundant presence, Jesus.

Hold (hands over heart):

Holy Spirit, in every shared prayer, you move powerfully.

Receive (hands open):

In our prayers, the Spirit moves, powerful and true.

SOULFUL BREATHING

Inhale deeply and feel your spirit aligning with others, a chorus of souls intertwined by his love. Envision the unity of believers, the collective strength found in his name. Feel his nearness, the reality of his Word advocating for communal faith.

Exhale deeply and release the burdens of isolation in that gentle breath. Let go of solitude's weight and enjoy the comforting presence of God's unwavering love.

Inhale: *When we gather in your name.*

Exhale: *You are among us.*

Conclude this soulful breathing in sacred stillness, allowing his promise to resonate within the innermost depths of your being. Gently sit in contemplative silence, inviting Scripture to settle within your heart and embracing its truth and peace.

SOULFUL REFLECTIONS

How does the knowledge that Christ is present in your gatherings change how you interact with fellow believers and approach communal worship?

In moments of solitude, how can you cultivate the same sense of divine presence Christ promised in communal prayer and fellowship?

CLOSING BENEDICTION

During shared prayers and heartfelt worship in your sacred gatherings, may you always find the comforting presence of the Lord, a guiding light illuminating your path. The unity of the Holy Spirit weaves a bond of peace and love among you, creating a sanctuary where you discern God's will and where his voice resonates with clarity and wisdom. May this divine fellowship nurture your spirit, fostering a deep sense of belonging and purpose. And in moments of trial and celebration alike, may the joy of the Lord be your unwavering strength, a steadfast source of courage as you journey together in faith. Welcome this journey, united with others in purpose and devotion, and let the love of Christ overflow in your hearts. In the name of Jesus, go forth in peace, carrying his love and light within you as a beacon of eternal hope to all you encounter. Amen.

Journal

Writing Thoughts and Prayers

"Write the vision;
make it plain on tablets,
so he may run who reads it."
HABAKKUK 2:2

In the stillness, you find a sanctuary for your soul, a haven where the whispers of God's voice are more apparent than the world's turmoil. Here, in the tranquil serenity, the words of Habakkuk resonate, urging you to write, not just to pen thoughts on paper but to etch God's truth onto the tablets of your heart.

In the quiet, you confront the madness of life's demands not with hurried steps but with holy contemplation. In the sacred act of journaling, you embark on a journey of spiritual introspection, where each word is a step closer to understanding God's will. Your words, thoughts, and prayers become the brushstrokes of a divine masterpiece.

In the sacred, the mundane words you jot down in your journal transform into prayers, rising like incense to the heavens. As you write, you realize you are sharing your thoughts with a God who listens intently to every word. Your journal becomes a collection of moments when you stood still long enough to share with the Father, Son, and Holy Spirit.

GUIDED MEDITATION

Focused Scriptural Meditation
Reflect on Habakkuk 2:2. Feel God's presence gently guiding you as the words of your journal take form.

Reflective Prayer and Listening
Invite the peace of his wisdom to fill you. Listen to him as he etches purpose on your soul.

Contemplation and Gratitude
Rest in the sacred space of God's love. Contemplate the vision he's revealing to you. Offer gratitude for the divine direction and the peace it brings to your life's path.

IMAGINATIVE CONTEMPLATION
As you stand on the balcony of an ancient tower under a celestial backdrop, the cool night air whispers secrets of old. The moonlight casts a silver glow, illuminating the parchment in your hands, a silent written testament to a promise whispered in the depths of your soul.

In this holy solitude, you feel a pivotal connection to the Divine. Your heart, a vessel of his wisdom, resonates with the eternal truth that his plans unfold. In this moment of holy stillness, you are more than a watcher; you are a bearer of a vision, a herald of a written divine promise. This scene, a vivid fabric of faith in writing, weaves into your being, forever changing your understanding of God's mysterious ways.

ECHOED VERSES

Hold (hands over heart):

Heavenly Father, your vision rests deep within my heart.

Receive (hands open):

I open myself to understand and accept your guidance.

Hold (hands over heart):

Lord Christ, in the stillness, I feel your presence, guiding me always.

Receive (hands open):

Receiving your wisdom, I walk confidently in your light.

Hold (hands over heart):

Holy Spirit, your guidance is a beacon in my journey. Guide me.

Receive (hands open):

With an open heart, I cherish your divine path for me.

SOULFUL BREATHING

Take in a slow breath, filling your lungs with the tranquility of God's presence. As you inhale, envision yourself receiving his vision, clear and pure. Hold this breath for a moment, letting the clarity of his purpose settle within you.

Now exhale slowly, releasing any doubts or fears. With each breath out, imagine making his vision plain, accessible, and understandable.

Inhale: *Show me your vision clearly.*

Exhale: *Help me reveal the truth.*

Now rest in a moment of stillness, allowing Habakkuk 2:2 to resonate in your heart and mind. Feel the transcendent peace and connection with God and carry this calm and clarity forward in your day.

SOULFUL REFLECTIONS

In what ways has God placed a vision in your heart, and how are you actively seeking to understand and share this vision in your daily life?

Reflect on the moments when you have felt most aligned with God's will. How can writing in your faith journal clarify his vision for you in these moments?

CLOSING BENEDICTION

May the Lord richly bless you with unmistakable clarity of vision and purpose, aligning your steps with his divine plan. In the mighty name of Jesus, may his wisdom guide you, illuminating your path with his truth. As you strive to express his vision, may strength and courage fill your heart, empowering your efforts. Let the peace of God, which transcends all understanding, guard your heart and mind in Christ Jesus. May you be wrapped in his love and grace with every step and stroke of the pen, and may he guide you in righteousness for his glory's sake. May you sense his presence in every challenge and triumph as you progress. In the name of Jesus, go in peace, encouraged to write your prayers, to love, and to serve the Lord with all your heart. Amen.

Worship

Celebrating God's Presence

Let everything that has breath praise the LORD!
Praise the LORD!
PSALM 150:6

In the stillness, you find yourself at the threshold of a sacred encounter. This is where the ebb and flow of life's demands fade, allowing space for your soul to expand. Your breath becomes a silent song of praise in this stillness, reminding you there is an opportunity for worship in every breath.

In the quiet, the clamor of daily life dims and ushers in a place of peace where the gentle whisper of God's voice becomes audible. Sacred praise echoes not as a loud exclamation but as a steady rhythm that aligns your heartbeat with the Divine. In the quiet, you realize that worship isn't always about human noise but is often about simply allowing God's voice to resound.

In the sacred, as you dwell in this holy rest, the kitchen table becomes an altar, the morning commute is a pilgrimage, and each act of kindness is a song. Here, in the sacred realm of everyday life, you realize that worship is not merely singing but also living a life that echoes the love of the Father, Son, and Holy Spirit.

GUIDED MEDITATION

Focused Scriptural Meditation

Let Psalm 150:6 resonate within you. Recognize that your existence is a precious melody in the Creator's grand symphony.

Reflective Prayer and Listening

Allow your prayer to be a loving invitation that calls forth a song from your soul. Sing your thoughts and feelings to God.

Contemplation and Gratitude

Let your heart fill with gratitude through silent yet sacred praise. Be one with the Divine, united as you offer him your endless worship.

IMAGINATIVE CONTEMPLATION

Imagine yourself in an ancient temple. The air vibrates with the strums of harps. The rhythm of tambourines and the soft patter of dancing feet blend in a rippling melody. Trumpets blare, each note a triumphant shout of adoration. In this sacred space, you stand amazed by the symphony of worship. Each instrument and voice converge for God's glory.

As you absorb this scene, your heart swells with a sense of belonging. You realize that your voice is an instrument, your life a song of praise. In this moment of spiritual intimacy, you find a deeper understanding of your purpose—to join in this cosmic chorus, celebrating the Creator's majesty with every breath, every action, every beat of your heart.

ECHOED VERSES

Hold (hands over heart):

Heavenly Father, my heart finds its steadfast beat in you.

Receive (hands open):

I welcome your peace, which fills me with divine breath.

Hold (hands over heart):

Lord Christ, your presence anchors my soul in serene trust.

Receive (hands open):

I embrace your love, which transforms my spirit with grace.

Hold (hands over heart):

Holy Spirit, because of your whispers, my fears dissolve.

Receive (hands open):

I receive your guidance, which leads me to eternal light.

SOULFUL BREATHING

Take a deep, slow breath, filling your lungs with the breath of life. As you inhale, silently acknowledge the presence of God around you. Hold this breath for a moment, cherishing the life he has given.

Now exhale slowly, releasing any tension or worry. With this breath, let go of anxieties and offer your praise to the Lord. Feel the rhythm of your breathing, a quiet echo of the words *Praise the Lord* within you.

Inhale: *Let everything that breathes.*

Exhale: *Praise the Lord.*

Inhale, recognizing and welcoming the love of God; exhale gently, releasing words of adoration. Feel your spirit intertwine more profoundly with his divine essence, each breath becoming a tender, heartfelt whisper of unwavering devotion and gratitude.

SOULFUL REFLECTIONS

In what ways does your daily life reflect a continuous song of praise to God, echoing the call of Psalm 150:6 to "praise the LORD"?

Reflect on the breath within you, a gift from the Creator. How does this awareness of your breath as a life-giving force from God inspire you to use it for his glory?

CLOSING BENEDICTION

In worship, may you encounter a holy connection to a divine chorus lifting an eternal melody. As every breath within you sings his praise, may your heart be tuned to the song of his love. May you find moments to rejoice in his presence, remembering that you move and have your being in him. During life's trials and triumphs, anchor your spirit in his unwavering faithfulness. May the peace of God, which surpasses all understanding, guard your heart, mind, and worship in Christ Jesus. Let each step you take reflect his grace and each word you speak echo his truth. And in the name of Jesus, go forth in joy to worship the Lord in all you do as a living testimony of his boundless love. Amen.

Nature

Praying in God's Creation

He waters the mountains from His upper chambers;
the earth is satisfied with the fruit of His works.
PSALM 104:13 AMP

In the stillness of nature, where the flurry of life falls silent, you find yourself alone with your thoughts and the Creator. Here God's handiwork whispers secrets of his eternal power. So still your heart and let worldly concerns fade away.

In the quiet of nature, you may perceive the turbulent demands of life diminish. In these peaceful moments, the voice of the Lord often becomes apparent, not as a thunderous roar but as a gentle whisper. Today's verse reveals God's creation; allow your heart to ponder this truth and rest in the tranquility of God's creation.

In the sacred space of nature, consider how God's hand is evident in every leaf, every star, and every breath of wind. In this holy recess, let your spirit acknowledge his omnipotence and omnipresence. This moment of stillness is not just a pause from the chaos but an opportunity to encounter the beauty and serenity of creation shaped by the Father, Son, and Holy Spirit.

GUIDED MEDITATION

Focused Scriptural Meditation
Reflect on Psalm 104:13 and feel God's masterpiece surrounding you.

Reflective Prayer and Listening
Speak to God in this sacred time, sharing your thoughts and feelings on every detail of creation.

Contemplation and Gratitude
In this moment, contemplate his magnificent creation and his constant care and offer thanks.

IMAGINATIVE CONTEMPLATION

Cradled under the night's firmament, you stand in the grandeur of creation. The sounds of the night whisper in a symphony of celestial wonder, each star a testament to God's eternal power and divinity. Here, in this hallowed stillness, even your own heartbeat echoes the divine truth that God's invisible attributes are manifest all around you.

Feel the awe and reverence over you as you stand amid the vastness of the heavens and the intricate beauty of the natural world. They each speak of the Creator's love and wisdom. In this sacred moment, you are not merely a witness to his glory but also a participant in the divine narrative. This contemplative journey deepens your connection with God, inviting you to explore the depths of your faith and find your place in the grand story of his creation.

ECHOED VERSES

Hold (hands over heart):

Heavenly Father, you reveal your power in creation's splendor.

Receive (hands open):

In awe, I ponder your majesty and grace.

Hold (hands over heart):

Lord Christ, in your love, the unseen becomes seen.

Receive (hands open):

I receive your love as it transforms my heart.

Hold (hands over heart):

Holy Spirit, help me perceive your divine nature.

Receive (hands open):

Open to your guidance, I walk in faith and truth.

SOULFUL BREATHING

With each deep breath, your lungs fill with the peace of God's presence. As you inhale, envision his eternal power surrounding you, uplifting you. Hold your breath briefly, contemplating the majesty of his divine nature as revealed in all creation.

Now gently exhale, allowing each slow breath to release the grip of doubts or fears. Feel the comforting warmth of his unwavering love envelop you like a soft blanket on a chilly evening, bringing peace and assurance.

Inhale: *Lord, you water mountains.*

Exhale: *Your earth is satisfied.*

Rest in this stillness, allowing the inspirational message of his eternal power and divinity to settle in your heart and mind. Feel the deep, abiding connection with your Creator in this sacred quiet.

SOULFUL REFLECTIONS

How does witnessing the intricacy and majesty of creation influence your understanding of God's eternal power and divinity?

How does the world around you reveal God's invisible qualities to you, and how do these perceptions inspire changes in your relationship with him?

CLOSING BENEDICTION

May the abundant grace of our Lord Jesus Christ be upon you, opening your eyes to the breathtaking splendor of God's creation. Gaze upon the wonders of the earth, from the rolling hills to the vibrant meadows, from the vast expanse of the heavens with stars like celestial jewels to the profound depths of the abyss, and let each wave whisper of his unfathomable grace and boundless mercy. As you journey through each day, may you walk in the radiant light of this truth, carrying the peace of the Lord within the sanctuary of your heart. May your faith be continually strengthened, your hope be enriched as a spring of living water, and your love overflow like a river. And now go with the joy of the Lord to love and serve in his glorious name. Embody his love in every word and every deed, for you are his precious child. In Jesus' name. Amen.

Meditate

Contemplating Deeper Truths

His delight is in the law of the LORD,
and on his law he meditates day and night.
PSALM 1:2

In the stillness of your heart, when the blaring world drifts to the background, you find an undisturbed space. It's a place where the soul breathes freely. In this stillness, you are invited to delve into the law of the Lord, which is not a set of rules but a wellspring of life-giving water.

In the quiet of these moments, communion with the Divine draws you. The law of the Lord transcends mere words. You are not just reading but also listening. You are absorbing and responding. The words are not just ink on paper but also life and breath. In the quiet, you understand that to meditate on his law is to weave his truth into your being.

In the sacred grip of his presence, meditating on his law is not a duty but a delight. Here, in the holy stillness, you are reminded that his law reflects his enduring character. As you meditate day and night, your life becomes a testament to the faithfulness of the Father, Son, and Holy Spirit.

GUIDED MEDITATION

Focused Scriptural Meditation

Let your heart delight in Psalm 1:2 and feel its wisdom refresh you like cool, flowing waters.

Reflective Prayer and Listening

Share your thoughts with God in this time of divine connection and listen for his guidance toward peace and wisdom.

Contemplation and Gratitude

Rest now, grateful for his eternal presence. Carry his peace and insights into your day.

IMAGINATIVE CONTEMPLATION

Imagine yourself in a lush garden beside a flowing river, its waters clear and steady. The river sustains a tree with deep roots and branches that reach to heaven in praise. The leaves of this tree rustle softly, each a testament to the enduring faithfulness of God. You imagine the gentle breeze as a divine caress, reminding you of God's constant presence.

The scene fills you with an overwhelming sense of peace and stability; God's Word nourishes you like the living waters nourish the tree. As you sit under the tree's canopy, you feel a sense of belonging cover you. You find clarity in this sacred space as you draw from the wellspring of God's love and grace. This garden, this tree, and this river are reflections of your spiritual journey, rooted and flourishing in the truth and love of God.

ECHOED VERSES

Hold (hands over heart):

Heavenly Father, you are my delight, day and night.

Receive (hands open):

I seize your truth as it fills my heart.

Hold (hands over heart):

Lord Christ, I find peace and joy in your law.

Receive (hands open):

Your wisdom guides me like a light on my path.

Hold (hands over heart):

Holy Spirit, your teachings are my constant meditation.

Receive (hands open):

I receive your insights and grow in your love.

SOULFUL BREATHING

Inhale deeply, immersing yourself in quiet meditation on God's enduring law. Allow his sacred Word to permeate every aspect of your being, filling you with divine wisdom and peace. As you hold this breath, let it be a moment of reflection to ponder his teachings and to find your soul nourished and filled by his unchanging truth.

Exhale slowly, releasing any tension or worry. Imagine yourself delighting more in God's Word, letting each beat of your heart be a meditation of his eternal truths.

Inhale: *I delight in your law.*

Exhale: *I meditate on it day and night.*

Continue this breathing pattern as each cycle draws you closer to embracing his Word. The steady rhythm prompts you to become enchanted with God's divine teachings.

SOULFUL REFLECTIONS

How does delighting in God's law transform your daily thoughts, decisions, and actions, bringing you closer to his heart?

In moments of silence and meditation, how do you experience the presence of God, and how does this deepen your understanding of his character and your relationship with him?

CLOSING BENEDICTION

May the Lord bless and keep you as you find joy and fulfillment in his law. May his Holy Word be a lamp unto your feet and a guiding light unto your path, illuminating the complexities of life with divine wisdom. In the quiet stillness of your heart, as the world fades away, may you meditate deeply on his eternal truths. Let these truths become a source of unshakable peace that flows through you. May the boundless grace of our Lord Jesus Christ enfold you in its warmth, the deep and abiding love of the Father envelop your soul, and the sweet fellowship of the Holy Spirit guide you in every step, decision, and moment, now and forever. Go forth in peace to love and diligently serve the Lord. Carry his Word in your heart, day and night, as a cherished treasure, a beacon of hope and love. Amen.

DAY 15

Intercede

Praying beyond Self

I urge that supplications, prayers, intercessions,
and thanksgivings be made for all people.
1 TIMOTHY 2:1

In the stillness, a holy voice invites you to journey beyond the
confines of your concerns, urging you to lift your eyes toward the
needs of others. Here you find the essence of true prayer as an
outpouring of supplication for yourself and all souls journeying
alongside you.

In the quiet, as the commotion of daily struggles fades behind
you, the hushed, holy voice sets the stage for a deeper communion in
the power of intercessory prayer. Like the gentle touch of a loving
hand, your prayers reach out to others' lives in unseen ways and
become bearers of God's love.

In the sacred space of intercession, you discover that your own
soul is nurtured and healed when you pray for others. As you lay
down healing words for those around you, your burdens lighten, and
your spirit soars. In this exchange, you discover that giving becomes
receiving, and as you lose yourself for others, you uncover a more
profound sense of who you are in the presence of the Father, Son, and
Holy Spirit.

GUIDED MEDITATION

Focused Scriptural Meditation

Reflect on 1 Timothy 2:1. Repeat the words as they resonate within you. Consider each word's significance.

Reflective Prayer and Listening

Intercede silently. Envision your prayers reaching other souls near and far.

Contemplation and Gratitude

Breathe in the divine connection with others, letting your thankful spirit rest in God's boundless love.

IMAGINATIVE CONTEMPLATION

Picture yourself in a vast, ancient hall. The soft murmurs of prayer fill the air. As a humble seeker in this sacred space, you are not alone but among the faithful. Each soul around you represents a life, a story, an earnest plea rising like incense to the heavens. The air carries the weight of collective supplication, yet an illuminating lightness resides here—the freedom that comes from laying down burdens for oneself and all humanity.

Feel the words of your prayer weaving into the lives of others, creating a beautiful melody that reaches the ears of God. In this act of intercession, you are connected not only to the Divine but also to the hearts of people you have never met. It's a reminder of the vastness of God's love, encompassing all, denying none.

ECHOED VERSES

Hold (hands over heart):

Heavenly Father, you accept everyone in love.

Receive (hands open):

I open my heart to your boundless grace.

Hold (hands over heart):

Lord Christ, your will reaches beyond me and touches lives everywhere.

Receive (hands open):

I accept the call to pray for others, God.

Hold (hands over heart):

Holy Spirit, your intercession inspires my humble prayers.

Receive (hands open):

In humility, I receive the strength to intercede.

SOULFUL BREATHING

Inhale deeply, allowing the tranquility of God's enduring presence to permeate your being. With each breath, silently consider the word *supplication*, feeling it resonate within you. Let this act become a sacred invitation, stirring your heart with an earnest desire to pray fervently for all people. This moment of intercession is an awe-inspiring connection with the Divine, so let it fill and satisfy your spirit.

Exhale slowly, releasing the word *intercession*, offering your heartfelt desires to God.

Inhale: *Supplication.*

Exhale: *Intercession.*

Continue this rhythmic breathing, letting each breath draw you closer to the truth of today's verse. Let the words settle in your heart and mind while you connect with the Divine. Conclude in stillness, resting in the calm and peace from this spiritual exercise.

SOULFUL REFLECTIONS

How can you extend your prayers beyond your needs to reflect God's all-encompassing love and concern for every soul?

How might your daily interactions and choices be transformed if you viewed each person you encounter as someone whom Jesus deeply cherishes and prays for?

CLOSING BENEDICTION

In this sacred moment, may you feel the holy unity in Christ that transcends your desires and connects you to others, a journey that sends you toward his lavish grace to all. May the Lord bless you deeply, covering you in his merciful grace. Let his countenance shine upon you, infusing your heart with the radiant light of his love. As you navigate life's hardships, may your prayers become a bridge of empathy, harmonizing with the chorus of petitions, intercessions, and gratitude for all souls. Let the peace of Christ govern your heart, steering you on paths of righteousness for the glory of his name. In every utterance and action, may you mirror the boundless generosity of Jesus, our cherished Lord and Savior. In the name of our beloved Jesus. Amen.

Explore

Discovering Different Ways of Prayer

[Pray] at all times in the Spirit, with all prayer and supplication.
To that end, keep alert with all perseverance,
making supplication for all the saints.
EPHESIANS 6:18

In the stillness, away from the chaotic paths of your day, a truth is
waiting for you to discover it. As the world fades away, you can find
yourself in the presence of something far greater than the sum of your
concerns. Here, in gentle solitude, you are invited to explore the depth
of your faith and commune with the Divine.

In the quiet, explore the varied ways of prayer, as diverse and
beautiful as the souls who whisper them. Ephesians 6 guides you,
urging prayer as a continual conversation with the one who knows
you best. In the quiet, you understand that prayer is not always about
asking but also about receiving, a sacred exchange where your heart
meets the holy.

In the sacred, tranquility is the holy suspension where your soul
catches its breath. Amid the stillness, quiet, and sacred, you discover a
journey of endless depth and wonder in the beauty of communion
with the Father, Son, and Holy Spirit.

GUIDED MEDITATION

Focused Scriptural Meditation

Reflect on Ephesians 6:18. Repeat and absorb the words as you connect with the heart of God.

Reflective Prayer and Listening

Open your heart to receive and give in an endless flow of prayer. With each breath, let the Holy Spirit fill and guide your prayer.

Contemplation and Gratitude

Rest in this silent, loving conversation with your Creator. Cherish this connection filled with gratitude for his endless love.

IMAGINATIVE CONTEMPLATION

Imagine yourself in a vast celestial space. Stars twinkle like diamonds in the night sky, each a testament to the Creator's majesty. In this cosmic splendor, you find yourself praying, your words weaving through creation and reaching the heart of God.

Feel the weight of your supplications, each an expression of your faith, hopes, and fears. As you pray, you are speaking not merely into the void but into the very essence of God.

In this sacred moment, it's as if heaven itself responds, affirming the significance of your every word, the depth of your every thought. This is the beauty of prayer: a mystical union between the human and the Divine, transcending time and space and bringing heaven to earth.

ECHOED VERSES

Hold (hands over heart):

Heavenly Father, you guide my heart to steadfast prayer.

Receive (hands open):

I open my soul to receive your endless grace.

Hold (hands over heart):

Lord Christ, in you I find strength for all times no matter where I am.

Receive (hands open):

Embracing your peace, I am renewed and deeply comforted.

Hold (hands over heart):

Holy Spirit, your whispers resonate in my devoted prayers.

Receive (hands open):

Your wisdom flows into me as a river of divine love.

SOULFUL BREATHING

Inhale deeply, absorbing the tranquility of God's presence. Silently ponder the words *praying at all times* as your breath draws in his peace. These words elevate your spirit, joining your soul with divine comfort and unwavering faith.

Now exhale slowly, releasing any tension or worries. Whisper in your heart, *In the Spirit*, feeling a deep connection with God. With each breath, you are drawing closer to his loving hold.

Inhale: *Praying at all times.*

Exhale: *In the Spirit.*

Reflect as this rhythm continues and you absorb the message of Ephesians 6:18 into the depths of your heart. Settle into the serenity, the spiritual connection, and the deep peace that flow from understanding and internalizing God's Word at all times.

SOULFUL REFLECTIONS

How can you practice praying at all times, embracing both the joys and challenges of life as opportunities to deepen your conversations with God?

How might keeping alert with all perseverance and sharing your innermost thoughts transform your understanding of God's presence and action in your life and in the lives of others?

CLOSING BENEDICTION

May the Lord bless you and keep you in his unending grace. As you live each day, let your heart be unwavering as you lift your voice to the Lord, continually tuned to heaven's gentle, guiding whispers. At every crossroads of life, whether it brings joy or trials, may you find the steadfast strength to persist. May you remain vigilant with a heart full of supplication, praying continuously for God's children. Now, in the sacred name of Jesus Christ, I pray that the peace of God, which surpasses all human understanding, will guard your heart and mind. May this divine peace lead you closer to his eternal, unfathomable love. And as you wake at first light and draw your first breath each day, may you know the assurance of his present love and guidance today and all the days to come. Amen.

Solitude

Spending Time Alone

Rising very early in the morning, while it was still dark,
he departed and went out to a desolate place, and there he prayed.
MARK 1:35

In the stillness of the early morning, just as the world begins to stir,
lies an opportunity for communion with the Divine. Here you can
walk the same path as Christ and seek a solitary place where troubles
cannot reach. Away from the torments you face, you can hear God's
gentle whispers in these moments.

In the quiet of solitude, your heart opens, ready to receive divine
wisdom. Here, away from the noise, you realize the power of solitude.
It is not merely the absence of sound but a chance to listen.

In this sacred moment, you discover you are never truly alone.
The creator of the universe meets you in these moments of seclusion,
wrapping you in a love that transcends time and space. In the hush of
the sacred, you meet the presence of the Father, Son, and Holy Spirit.

GUIDED MEDITATION

Focused Scriptural Meditation

Reflect on Mark 1:35 as your heart finds a sacred space for communion in solitude.

Reflective Prayer and Listening

Pray calmly. Let your soul experience God's nearness, understanding, and peace.

Contemplation and Gratitude

In this moment of solitude, dwell in gratitude. Acknowledge the peace and presence of God in your life.

IMAGINATIVE CONTEMPLATION

Imagine yourself walking alongside Jesus. The world is still, as if holding its breath in the serenity before daybreak. Your feet tread softly on the wet grass, following him to a secluded place, a refuge untouched by the day's impending racket.

In this holy quiet, you witness his communion with the Father, an intimate exchange between heaven and earth. You feel the air thick with the presence of the Divine, a tangible weight of holy whispers and unseen embraces. As Jesus prays, sense the depth of the divine dialogue that transcends words.

This scene is a testament to the power of prayer in solitude. Jesus turns and offers you a sacred invitation to seek your own place of solitude, to find him in the quiet where his voice is more evident, his presence nearer, and the evidence of his love even more soul stirring.

ECHOED VERSES

Hold (hands over heart):

Heavenly Father, I rise early, seeking solitude in the quiet.

Receive (hands open):

I seek your presence in the stillness of my heart.

Hold (hands over heart):

Lord Christ, through your example, prayer becomes a sacred, solitary refuge.

Receive (hands open):

Teach me to find peace in the quiet dawn hours.

Hold (hands over heart):

Holy Spirit, you whisper in silence and solitude, guiding me to listen.

Receive (hands open):

In this solitary hush, I hear your voice, feel your love, and accept your guidance.

SOULFUL BREATHING

As you settle, inhale deeply, reflecting on Jesus, who found solitude before daybreak. Hold this breath, feeling the tranquility of his presence.

Gently exhale and imitate how he abandoned earthly ties to commune with the Father. Accept this moment of stillness just as he did in his sacred morning rituals, allowing his peace to saturate your very being.

Inhale: *Jesus, I pray to you.*

Exhale: *In this solitary place.*

Rest in this solitude as you breathe this cycle, allowing today's verse to resonate within you, bringing a reverential sense of connection with God. Stay in this moment of stillness, held by his eternal love.

SOULFUL REFLECTIONS

In the quiet moments before dawn, in what ways do you find your heart wandering, and how might seeking solitude, as Jesus did, transform your communion with God?

Reflect on how Jesus intentionally retreated to a lonely place for prayer. What distractions do you need to step away from to deepen your connection with God?

CLOSING BENEDICTION

In the quiet presence of tranquil solitude, may your soul unfurl and find a sanctuary where your spirit dances to the rhythm of God's heartbeat. Clothed in this serene presence, carry this connection with the Creator through your day. As dawn breaks in the hush of early morning, may you venture to a solitary place to pray. Let the peace of the Lord Christ accompany you wherever he sends you. May he navigate you through the wilderness, shield you in storms, and lead you home as you rejoice in the wonders he reveals. With your every step, may his guidance be your compass, strength, and support. Return home not just to a place but also to a state of grace, where joy overflows at the marvels you have witnessed. In the name of Jesus, may you find your journey and your destination. Amen.

DAY 18

Battles

Praying for Protection

We do not wrestle against flesh and blood, but against the rulers,
against the authorities, against the cosmic powers over this present
darkness, against the spiritual forces of evil in the heavenly places.
EPHESIANS 6:12

In the stillness, a sublime peace transcends the turmoil of your
worldly battles. As you sit in silence, remember that your struggles are
not against flesh and blood but against spiritual forces beyond your
perception. You are not just a bystander but a warrior, clad in the
armor of God and shielded by his unending grace.

In the quiet, as you feel the calm, let your heart reflect on the
reality that your battles are fought and won not by physical might but
through spiritual strength, not with a loud cry but with a whispered
prayer.

In the sacred, you find a connection to the Divine that is both
intimate and powerful. Prayerful stillness created this holy space,
reminding you of the eternal truth that a force far more significant
than any earthly power guides you. Here you can find rest and
refreshment, confident that your spiritual armor is offered and
fortified by the Father, Son, and Holy Spirit.

GUIDED MEDITATION

Focused Scriptural Meditation

Read Ephesians 6:12. Visualize standing firm, shielded in God's mighty protection.

Reflective Prayer and Listening

In this state of worship, feel around you the strength of his armor that dispels all fear. He is a shield against the invisible.

Contemplation and Gratitude

In God's presence, rest grateful in this assurance that his protection is unending.

IMAGINATIVE CONTEMPLATION

Picture yourself standing in an ethereal realm, the air pulsating with unseen battles. Divine protection armors you: a breastplate of righteousness, a helmet of salvation, the gospel of peace grounding your feet. In your hand, the sword of the Spirit, God's Word, gleams, sharp and unyielding.

Feel the weight of the shield of faith in your hand as you deflect fiery darts, each a temptation along this earthly journey. Your heart beats with a rhythm of unwavering faith in God's glory.

This scene is not a fantasy but a vivid illustration of your spiritual warfare. In this contemplation, realize the magnitude of God's power within you, a strength surpassing all earthly bounds. Remember that in every challenge, you are not alone; the Almighty equips and empowers you.

ECHOED VERSES

Hold (hands over heart):

> *Heavenly Father, you guard my heart in unseen battles.*

Receive (hands open):

> *I accept your protection, feeling peace within.*

Hold (hands over heart):

> *Lord Christ, your strength shields me from hidden foes.*

Receive (hands open):

> *With an open heart, I receive your unwavering courage.*

Hold (hands over heart):

> *Holy Spirit, guide me through spiritual darkness.*

Receive (hands open):

> *With open hands, I welcome your guiding light.*

SOULFUL BREATHING

Breathe in the awareness of God's presence around you. Envision drawing in God's strength and peace as you inhale. Hold this breath momentarily, acknowledging the battles unseen, the spiritual forces beyond your sight.

Now slowly exhale. With each breath out, release your fears, your doubts, and the weight of the invisible battles you face. Feel the lightness as you surrender these to God.

Inhale: *Strength in heavenly realms.*

Exhale: *Triumph over dark forces.*

As you repeat this exercise, let Ephesians 6 continue to echo within you. Conclude each cycle with a moment of stillness as you absorb these reflections into your heart. In these sacred pauses, feel a deep connection with God, finding unparalleled inner peace in his presence. Let this soulful breathing transform and uplift you, strengthening your spiritual journey.

SOULFUL REFLECTIONS

In light of the unseen spiritual struggles described in Ephesians 6:12, reflect on your daily life. Where do you sense the most need for God's strength and guidance?

How can you deepen your spiritual practices, such as prayer and meditation on God's Word, to better discern and withstand these invisible influences?

CLOSING BENEDICTION

On the spiritual battleground, we do not contend against mere flesh and blood but against formidable rulers, authorities, and cosmic powers residing in this present darkness and against the spiritual forces of evil in heavenly realms. In Jesus' mighty name, may the Lord guide you through the complexities and challenges of this earthly battleground. Let the strength and wisdom of God be your unwavering guide, his peace your protective shield, and his enduring love your constant companion. In every trial and tribulation, may you discover courage and comfort, knowing that his presence is ever near. May the Holy Spirit empower you, divine grace uphold you, and unshakable hope inspire you as you walk steadfastly in the light of Christ. Proceed in peace, fortified by determined faith and deeply enriched by Jesus' eternal, encompassing love. Amen.

Forgiveness

Releasing and Letting Go

"If you forgive others their trespasses, your heavenly Father will also
forgive you, but if you do not forgive others their trespasses,
neither will your Father forgive your trespasses."
MATTHEW 6:14–15

In the stillness, when the world's commotion fades, your heart
becomes a sanctuary for divine whispers. In this serene and holy
space, you find the courage to face the most challenging human task:
forgiveness. Listen for the soft, insistent voice of the Lord, reminding
you of the freedom to let go.

In the quiet, a profound mystery invites you to ponder the power of
forgiveness. Forgiveness brings light to the shadows of your soul. It is
not just a gift you offer others but a divine key that unlocks your chains.

In the sacred stillness, you understand the true essence of
forgiveness. It's an act, a journey, a decision, and a daily practice.
Here, in the presence of the Almighty, you grasp that to forgive is to
mirror the heart of your heavenly Father. Each act of forgiveness is a
step closer to the person God has called you to be, a step toward the
Father, Son, and Holy Spirit.

GUIDED MEDITATION

Focused Scriptural Meditation

As you consider Matthew 6:14–15, focus on how God has forgiven you and how you need to forgive others.

Reflective Prayer and Listening

In this quiet moment with your Forgiver, offer forgiveness for each person you've encountered, especially where hurt exists.

Contemplation and Gratitude

Accept the peace of his forgiveness and offer thanks as you feel your heavenly Father's love renew your spirit.

IMAGINATIVE CONTEMPLATION

Imagine yourself on a sunlit hillside. Before you, Jesus speaks to a crowd, his voice a melody of wisdom and truth. As he unfolds the mysteries of the kingdom, your heart resonates with his words about forgiveness.

In the crowd, see the faces of those you need to forgive. Hear the whisper of the Holy Spirit urging you to release the chains of resentment. Jesus' words seep into the parched soil of your soul, nurturing seeds of grace and understanding.

In this moment, the Divine and human intertwine, revealing the eternal beauty of forgiveness. It's a sacred echo in your heart, a call to allow love over bitterness, transforming your spirit and deepening your communion with God. This vibrant and spirited scene invites a journey of both the mind and the soul, where each step toward forgiveness is a step closer to the Divine.

ECHOED VERSES

Hold (hands over heart):

Heavenly Father, I ask you for your forgiveness from the depths of my heart.

Receive (hands open):

I open my heart to the transformative power of your grace.

Hold (hands over heart):

Lord Christ, teach me to release resentment and hold on to peace.

Receive (hands open):

Receiving your peace, I let go of all my burdens.

Hold (hands over heart):

Holy Spirit, may you guide me in the path of forgiveness.

Receive (hands open):

With open hands, I accept the gift of your mercy.

SOULFUL BREATHING

Breathe in God's boundless grace, filling your lungs with forgiveness. Hold your breath gently within you.

As you exhale, release any resentment you harbor, letting go of the burdens on your heart. Feel the release of your transgressions, washed away by divine mercy.

Inhale: *Forgiveness liberates my soul.*

Exhale: *Love embraces. Healing follows.*

Deepen your connection to God's love and grace with every breathing cycle. As you rest in stillness, let forgiveness and mercy resonate deeply within you. Feel his presence envelop your soul, offering peace and understanding. In this quiet moment, find strength in his unending mercy as you release burdens and welcome divine love.

SOULFUL REFLECTIONS

How might embracing forgiveness as a reflection of God's love transform your relationships and deepen your connection with the Lord?

In what ways can the practice of forgiving others reveal new dimensions of your heavenly Father's mercy and grace in your life?

CLOSING BENEDICTION

May the Lord Jesus Christ enclose you in his arms of grace, steering your steps toward forgiveness and love. As you feel his hold, release resentment and accept God's transformative grace. Let this divine act foster a sanctuary of understanding, nurturing your spirit as you journey through complicated relationships. In gratitude, recognize the life-enhancing beauty and vibrancy this grace yields. Let the heavenly Father fortify you with the strength to let go of grievances, echoing his forgiveness. May his Spirit light your way, guiding you to deeper awareness and empathy for others. In moments of doubt, may you seek solace in his boundless mercy. Allow his love to be your protector, his wisdom your navigator, his forgiveness your constant support. As you follow his path, let your heart mirror his infinite grace, affecting others' lives with the same forgiveness you've received. In Jesus' name, proceed in peace and joy, cradled in his everlasting love. Amen.

DAY 20

Bless

Forwarding Prayers of Blessing

"The LORD bless you and keep you;
the LORD make his face to shine upon you and be gracious to you;
the LORD lift up his countenance upon you and give you peace."
NUMBERS 6:24–26

In the stillness, where the rhythm of your heart aligns with God, there lies an unfathomable blessing. In these moments, away from life's demands, you find a sanctuary where the Lord's blessings become not just words from ancient Scripture but a living reality.

In the quiet, you discover you can genuinely absorb the divine nuances of God's love. As the Lord's face shines upon you, you feel the warmth of his blessings illuminating the corners of your heart. Here the Lord lifts his face toward you, and in that holy gaze, you find an unspoken promise of peace that surpasses all understanding.

In the sacred, you realize the Lord's blessings allow you to continuously walk with him, each step presenting an opportunity to be a vessel of God's grace to those around you. To bless others in a world yearning for a divine touch is to show the love of the Father, Son, and Holy Spirit.

GUIDED MEDITATION

Focused Scriptural Meditation

Reflect on Numbers 6:24–26 and feel the loving gaze of the Lord upon you.

Reflective Prayer and Listening

As you pour out your heart to the Almighty, share your thoughts and listen for his voice and the promise of his eternal care.

Contemplation and Gratitude

Rest in his peace and thankfully acknowledge that you are held, cherished, and infinitely blessed in this sacred moment.

IMAGINATIVE CONTEMPLATION

Envision yourself in an expansive valley, the gentle breeze whispering God's secrets through the sounds of leaves, streams, and birdsong. In this sacred space, you sense his gaze upon you like the warm glow of evening light.

In this serene landscape, you feel a connection to the Creator as the stars emerge in the twilight sky. His numerous blessings descend upon you like a gentle rain. Each drop is a promise of peace that seeps into the soil of your soul, nurturing seeds of hope.

This moment transcends time, a holy communion with the Divine. As you stand in the valley, bathed in the celestial lights, your heart echoes with a deep understanding of God's boundless grace. In this contemplative moment, you find solace in the eternal glow of God's face and his smile upon you.

ECHOED VERSES

Hold (hands over heart):

Heavenly Father, you always hold me in your loving arms.

Receive (hands open):

I receive your grace, a gift of unending love.

Hold (hands over heart):

Lord Christ, I find peace and solace in your light.

Receive (hands open):

Your light fills me, guiding my path through darkness.

Hold (hands over heart):

Holy Spirit, your presence is always comforting and constant.

Receive (hands open):

I welcome your presence, feeling peace and divine connection.

SOULFUL BREATHING

As you breathe, close your eyes and feel your spirit revitalize. With each inhale, envision the Lord's face shining upon you, a warm, comforting light.

Exhale slowly, releasing any tension and trusting in his protection. Feel his grace wash over you and leave tranquility in its wake.

Inhale: *Lord, bless me.*

Exhale: *As your face shines upon me.*

Adopt God's divine peace and love while you breathe in this serene moment. Allow these emotions to linger as you hold your breath. Gently open your eyes and carry this calmness with you, feeling refreshed and deeply connected to his divine presence. This stillness is a blessing, a gift from above that is infused in your heart and soul and endures beyond this quiet moment.

SOULFUL REFLECTIONS

How does the assurance of God's blessing, as depicted in today's verses, shape your understanding of his presence and providence in your daily life?

In your faith journey, how can you embody and reflect to those around you the peace and grace that the Lord extends to you?

CLOSING BENEDICTION

May the Lord bless you and keep you, holding you close in his tender care. Let his face shine upon you, illuminating your path with the light of his smiling countenance. In his graciousness, may you discover the truly penetrating depths of his love and mercy, a sanctuary for your mind, body, soul, and spirit. As you navigate each day, may the Lord reveal himself to you, bestowing upon you a peace that transcends all understanding and steadies the heart in every circumstance. In your life's journey, through moments of joy and times of trial, may you always feel the comfort of his eternal presence. And now, in the sacred name of Jesus, step forward, carrying the assurance of his blessing. Go into the world as a bearer of his peace and love and a reflection of his light. Amen.

DAY 21

Partners

Sharing in Prayerful Support

Two are better than one,
because they have a good reward for their toil.
For if they fall, one will lift up his fellow.
ECCLESIASTES 4:9–10

In the stillness of your heart, ponder the beautiful truth of companionship in Christ. How incredible that the partnership is both a blessing and a divine provision in your spiritual journey. In this moment, reflect on the assurance that a kindred spirit in faith is a tangible manifestation of God's love working through his people.

In the quiet of your soul, consider the times of solitude when you've stumbled, longing for a hand to lift you. The voice of God often speaks through the presence of a friend, so in times of vulnerability, the truth of Ecclesiastes becomes evident—that partnership in faith is not merely about physical support but also about spiritual sustenance.

In the sacred space, recognize the holiness of relationships born in faith. The sacredness of these bonds transcends the ordinary, turning every shared prayer and word of encouragement into a living testimony of divine grace, an extension of the love of the Father, Son, and Holy Spirit.

GUIDED MEDITATION

Focused Scriptural Meditation
Contemplate Ecclesiastes 4:9–10. Consider a word from this passage
that touches your heart and allow its meaning to resonate within you.

Reflective Prayer and Listening
Share with God your thoughts and feelings about your relationships.
Listen for his gentle guidance.

Contemplation and Gratitude
Rest in the assurance of God's presence. Thank him for the care he
offers through the comfort of others.

IMAGINATIVE CONTEMPLATION

Imagine yourself in an ancient, bustling, sun-drenched marketplace
outside the court of King Solomon. You see a laborer, his brow
furrowed in exertion as he endlessly toils alone. His solitude contrasts
with a pair of workers nearby. Their laughter mingles as they share
their efforts, each lightening the other's load.

As you observe this scene, recognize that the solitary worker
embodies the emptiness of singular toil and serves as a poignant
reminder of our innate need for companionship. In contrast, the pair's
joyful collaboration speaks to the strength and comfort found in
fellowship with both other humans and the Divine.

This scene invites you to reflect on your life, the moments of
lonely struggle and the grace of shared journeys. It is a gentle nudge
to cherish the companions God provides and to be that companion to
others, embodying the love and support that echoes his presence in
our lives.

ECHOED VERSES

Hold (hands over heart):

> *Heavenly Father, you are my strength when I stand alone.*

Receive (hands open):

> *In fellowship, I find support that lifts me from solitude.*

Hold (hands over heart):

> *Lord Christ, my toil finds purpose and reward in your companionship.*

Receive (hands open):

> *When I have a friend, every fall is met with a helping hand.*

Hold (hands over heart):

> *Holy Spirit, show me how to cherish the bonds you provide.*

Receive (hands open):

> *In unity, burdens lighten, and we reflect your divine love, God.*

SOULFUL BREATHING

As you inhale, envision God's presence wrapping around you, bringing strength through togetherness. Hold this breath, feeling the unity and support it represents.

Now exhale any sense of solitude or burden, imagining God raising you up just as you might lift a companion in their time of need.

Inhale: *Together, we achieve more.*

Exhale: *Companionship lifts me.*

Continue this breathing rhythm, absorbing the truth that unity surpasses isolation. Gently breathe, releasing your breath into the calm and letting the wisdom of Ecclesiastes resonate in your heart. Rest in this peaceful moment, feeling a deep connection with God. Cherish this serene spiritual harmony surrounded by God's loving presence.

SOULFUL REFLECTIONS

How have you experienced God's presence in the form of human relationships, and how have these relationships mirrored his love and strength in your life?

How might you actively seek to support and encourage others as a reflection of God's love and purpose in your life?

CLOSING BENEDICTION

In your journey, know that you do not walk alone. The Lord, in his infinite wisdom, offers the blessing of companionship. It is a divine promise that two united in purpose and faith wield greater strength. May his grace, ever abundant, empower you to seamlessly be both a bearer of sorrow in times of trial and receiver of delight in happy moments. The encompassing love of Christ is soothing, easing your burdens and magnifying your joy. So may this divine companionship be your steadfast guide, nurturing a spirit that willingly offers support and humbly accepts it. In Jesus' hallowed name, receive the world with a heart at peace. May you know that you are deeply loved, known, and seen, and within the hallowed union of divine fellowship, may you find strength unimagined. Remember that in every step, the Lord is with you, his presence a constant source of comfort and courage. Amen.

Promises

Standing on God's Word

He has granted to us his precious and very great promises,
so that through them you may become partakers of the divine nature.
2 PETER 1:4

In the stillness, where the world's commotion dissolves into a hush,
God's divine nature resonates with a clarity untouched by the
betrayals of daily life. As the world rushes by, you stand anchored,
feeling each heartbeat as a testament to his enduring presence and
promises. This stillness is your refuge, a place where God's covenant
voice emerges.

In the quiet, away from the swirl of your day, you can discover a
holy pause. Here God invites you to ponder the depths of his
covenant. Like a tree planted by streams of water, you draw strength
and nourishment for your soul from the richness of his Word.

In the sacred, God's promises become more than words; they
weave into the very fabric of your being. As you dwell in his holiness,
let the assurance of his Word swaddle you like a blanket. His promises
shine like stars in the night sky, each a testament to the unending
faithfulness and love of the Father, Son, and Holy Spirit.

GUIDED MEDITATION

Focused Scriptural Meditation

Reflect on 2 Peter 1:4. Feel the Lord's loving gaze binding your being and his promises casting away shadows of doubt and fear.

Reflective Prayer and Listening

As you rest in his presence, share your thoughts with him. Listen for his whispered promises of eternal care. Know that you are held, cherished, and infinitely blessed.

Contemplation and Gratitude

In this sacred moment, let peace fill your heart. Acknowledge the tranquility the Father brings and offer thanks for his unfailing love and promised presence in your life.

IMAGINATIVE CONTEMPLATION

Picture yourself standing in a landscape bathed in the soft light of dawn, the horizon aglow with promise. You feel the warmth of the sun's first rays, a reminder of God's enduring faithfulness.

Around you, the world awakens, each stirring creature exhibiting God's magnificent creation. In this moment, you are acutely aware of God's presence, as real as the earth beneath your feet. You feel anchored and present in his creation. You reflect on his promises, each a brushstroke on the masterpiece that is your life, each painting a future filled with hope and purpose. This scene fills you with gratitude and awe, deepening your connection to the Divine.

ECHOED VERSES

Hold (hands over heart):

Heavenly Father, I find my strength in your promises.

Receive (hands open):

Your unwavering faithfulness renews me.

Hold (hands over heart):

Lord Christ, your Word lights my path, guiding me forward.

Receive (hands open):

In your light, I walk confidently and peacefully.

Hold (hands over heart):

Holy Spirit, my soul finds rest in your whispered guarantees.

Receive (hands open):

I am whole, secure, and loved in your divine presence.

SOULFUL BREATHING

Inhale deeply, drawing in the certainty of God's promises. Let his words fill your lungs and spread peace throughout your being.

Exhale slowly, releasing any doubt so his promises become part of you. Inhale faith and exhale worry.

Inhale: *In faith, I partake of you.*

Exhale: *Your promises are true.*

Continue this cycle. Inhale deeply, feeling his presence. With each exhale, sense his assurances reverberating in your soul. Persist in this rhythmic breathing, letting his words echo within. Conclude in tranquil stillness, allowing his comforting promises to nestle into your heart. Remain there, embracing the unwavering love and constant presence of the Divine. In this sacred moment, find solace and strength, knowing that he is ever near and that his love is unceasing.

SOULFUL REFLECTIONS

How have God's promises been a refuge in your times of struggle?

Reflect on a moment when you felt God's promises come alive. What changed within you?

CLOSING BENEDICTION

Let this prayer be a sanctuary for your heart, a reminder of the venerable connection between the Creator and his creation. May it inspire a deeper faith and a more intimate walk with the Lord as you navigate the complexities of life with his eternal wisdom guiding your steps. In this serene moment, let your spirit gently awaken to his divine whispers, those promises that resonate across time and space. God bestows his precious and magnificent promises upon you so you may partake in his divine essence. As you bask in the stillness of your being, find assurance in his unchanging promises, as certain as the constant cycle of the seasons. May his Word illuminate your path, a steadfast lamp amid this world's shadows. In Jesus' blessed name, walk with the unwavering certainty of his love as your life radiates the brilliance of his eternal truth. Receive the blessing of fortitude to cling to his promises and the insight to discern his workings in every segment of your life's tableau. Amen.

Fasting

Seeking God Sacrificially

"When you fast, anoint your head and wash your face, that your
fasting may not be seen by others but by your Father who is in secret.
And your Father who sees in secret will reward you."

MATTHEW 6:17–18

In the stillness of fasting, you encounter a whispering presence, a
gentle divine tug drawing you away from discomfort. Time pauses in
this holy moment of solitude.

In the quiet, your heart begins to resonate with the eternal. Here,
away from any apprehension, you hear the soft murmur of God's voice.
You discern the true essence of your faith in these hushed interludes.
Like the serene surface of a still lake, your soul reflects the beauty of a
deeper understanding, an intimate connection with the Divine.

In the sacred, you encounter God in the whisper. The world
demands your attention, but it is in this secret holy pause that you
find true fulfillment. As Elijah discovered God not in the earthquake
or fire but in the gentle whisper, so do these quiet, sacred moments of
introspection and surrender found in fasting reveal the Father, Son,
and Holy Spirit.

GUIDED MEDITATION

Focused Scriptural Meditation

Ponder Matthew 6:17–18, letting each word resonate in your heart and sink deeply into your soul.

Reflective Prayer and Listening

In this time of intimate exchange, share your thoughts and feelings with God and find time to listen, welcoming his guidance and wisdom as you fast.

Contemplation and Gratitude

Rest in the knowledge of God's constant presence and offer thanks for his provision.

IMAGINATIVE CONTEMPLATION

Visualize a simple room, dimly lit by a single flickering candle that casts soft shadows on the walls. You sit quietly on a carved wooden chair and contemplate the purpose of your fast—simplicity and sacrifice. The aroma of uneaten bread lingers in the air, a temptation that tugs at your senses. Your choice is clear—to feast on spiritual nourishment rather than physical sustenance.

Your stomach growls, an echo in the silent room, but your heart swells with a deeper hunger, a yearning for divine intimacy. Each rumble is a stark reminder of your physical needs, yet it pales when compared to your spiritual longing. You realize this hunger is a symbol of your dependence on God, a physical manifestation of a spiritual journey, and a tangible act of worship.

ECHOED VERSES

Hold (hands over heart):

Heavenly Father, you reveal your boundless grace in your stillness.

Receive (hands open):

I open my heart to receive your unending love.

Hold (hands over heart):

Lord Christ, in your silence, you speak volumes about your faithfulness.

Receive (hands open):

I hold on to your words, letting them fulfill and sustain me.

Hold (hands over heart):

Holy Spirit, in your sacrifice, you show the depths of your love.

Receive (hands open):

I accept your portion, and I am filled and deeply satisfied by your presence.

SOULFUL BREATHING

Inhale, feeling God's presence filling and satisfying you. Each breath in through your nose reminds you of the humility of fasting.

Exhale, releasing doubts or fears and surrendering your desires to his care. With each breath, reflect on the emptiness you feel in your body, a sacrifice you make to draw nearer to the Lord.

Inhale: *I fast humbly and quietly.*

Exhale: *God, you reward openly and joyfully.*

Continue breathing as your heart aligns with his, letting faith and trust grow within your spirit. Feel his love and grace settling in you, fostering serene confidence and a divine connection. This rhythm gently harmonizes your being with the Divine, creating an intimate, peaceful bond with him.

SOULFUL REFLECTIONS

In what ways has the practice of fasting brought you closer to understanding God's heart and his plans for you?

How has the sacrifice of denying yourself physical comfort deepened your appreciation for Christ's ultimate sacrifice and love?

CLOSING BENEDICTION

Consider the soaring birds, unfettered by worry, a testament to the peace that awaits you as God sustains you in fasting. Anoint your head and wash your face as you fast so that your fasting may be seen not by others but by only your Father. And your Father, who sees what is done in secret, will reward you. May the Lord's peace provide for and go with you. May he guide and protect you through the wilderness of earthly desires and temptations. May he bring you home as you rejoice at the provision he has shown you. In the name of Jesus, may his light illuminate your path, his wisdom fill your mind, and his peace reign in your heart. As you walk in his footsteps, may you be blessed with the courage to face each challenge and the grace to celebrate each joy. Go now in the assurance of his unfailing love, for he is with you now and always. Amen.

Kneel

Exploring Prayerful Traditions

He got down on his knees three times a day and prayed
and gave thanks before his God, as he had done previously.
DANIEL 6:10

In the stillness, you find yourself enveloped in a divine gentleness, away from the whirlwind of life's demands. It's here, in the still sanctuary of your soul, where the whispers of the Divine gently stir you. In these moments of stillness, kneel before the one who cradles you in arms of grace.

In the quiet, the world's noise fades into a lullaby, and in its place, the soothing rhythm of your heartbeat echoes a sacred song. You remember Daniel, unwavering in his faith, who found solace and strength on his knees. His practice of stillness is a peaceful testament to the steadfastness of faith amid life's tumult.

In the sacred pause, you find a space of holy communion to kneel where heaven and earth seem to touch. It's a sacred, physical response; you are led not by ritual but by humility, following the gentle rhythm of the Father, Son, and Holy Spirit.

GUIDED MEDITATION

Focused Scriptural Meditation

As you reflect on Daniel 6:10, let the words echo within you. Kneel in the presence of God, which surrounds you.

Reflective Prayer and Listening

In this moment of stillness, share your heart with God. Release your worries and bow humbly in his encompassing grace.

Contemplation and Gratitude

In this sacred contemplation, simply be with God. In gratitude, carry his peace and assurance with you all day.

IMAGINATIVE CONTEMPLATION

Envision yourself in an upper chamber, the golden light of dawn bathing the room. You kneel. The coolness of the stone floor is a gentle reminder of the sacred ground on which you rest.

Outside, the world slowly stirs to life, its myriad sounds a distant murmur against the hallowed silence of your sanctuary. Within these walls, time ceases to dictate your thoughts; instead, eternity whispers. You are kneeling in the presence of the Almighty.

In this serene communion, you find a haven of peace as you kneel, a crossroads of the holy and the mortal, the sacred and the secular. This act of kneeling, of bowing in reverence, becomes a powerful symbol of your devotion, a bridge that connects your heart to the heart of the Divine.

ECHOED VERSES

Hold (hands over heart):

Heavenly Father, you hold me close in your steadfast love.

Receive (hands open):

I receive your peace, which surpasses all understanding.

Hold (hands over heart):

Lord Christ, your grace encircles me like a shield of strength.

Receive (hands open):

In quiet trust, I embrace your guidance.

Hold (hands over heart):

Holy Spirit, you whisper the truth. In stillness, I hear you.

Receive (hands open):

Your Word is a lamp to my feet, lighting my path.

SOULFUL BREATHING

Kneel and, as you breathe in, imagine the steadfast faith of Daniel, who remained unwavering and trustworthy. Inhale the courage to stand firm in your faith, strong in the face of uncertainty.

Exhale slowly and release uncertainty and doubt as Daniel did when facing trials. With each breath, feel your connection with God deepen, your heart aligning with his.

Inhale: *Daniel knelt and prayed daily.*

Exhale: *Give me faith in uncertainty.*

In every breathing cycle, whisper a prayer, engaging in quiet communion with God. In this serene moment, allow Scripture to permeate your heart. Experience a deep peace and connection with the Divine. This sacred practice transforms each breath into a prayerful acceptance of God's presence.

SOULFUL REFLECTIONS

How might embodying stillness in your daily life deepen your connection with God, as it did for Daniel?

In moments of challenge, how can kneeling before God, like Daniel did, transform your perspective and strengthen your faith?

CLOSING BENEDICTION

May the peace of the Lord Christ enfold you, accompanying you wherever he may graciously lead. May his divine guidance be your compass through the uncharted wilderness of your days, and may his unfailing strength be your shield through your fiercest storms. As you journey forward, may you find your way home, celebrating the marvels he has revealed as your heart overflows with joy. As you stand again at welcoming doors, may your return be a time of rejoicing, a testament to the Lord's enduring faithfulness. In the hallowed name of Jesus, kneel and let your heart be a place of endless love for God. Let this love reflect the steadfast faith of Daniel, which was unwavering in the face of adversity, and let it be your guiding light, leading you along life's journey. May it shine brightly, revealing the path with the radiance of his grace and truth. Amen.

Artistry

Creating Prayer through Art

> "He has filled [Bezalel] with the Spirit of God…
> and with all craftsmanship, to devise artistic designs,
> to work in gold and silver and bronze."
> EXODUS 35:31–32

In the stillness, you find yourself amid a world that often whirls in relentless motion, but the cacophony of life's demands fades in this peaceful sanctuary, allowing your soul time to breathe. During these moments of serenity, listen to the gentle cadence of God's voice speaking into the depths of your being.

In the quiet, the creative heart meets the Divine. In this tranquil, artistic oasis, your spirit is nurtured and replenished. Remember the beauty of simply being, of existing in the presence of the one who knows and loves you unconditionally.

In the sacred, the Master's hand touches the depth of your soul. As you sit in his presence, you become aware of the intricate framework of your life, which the Lord has woven with glistening threads of love. In these moments of contemplative reverence, you realize the divine creative expression at work within you, crafting a masterpiece that reflects the splendor of the Father, Son, and Holy Spirit.

GUIDED MEDITATION

Focused Scriptural Meditation

Reflect on Exodus 35:31–32. Feel the artistry of God surround you with divine creative energy.

Reflective Prayer and Listening

As you express your deepest desires, feel the Holy Spirit guiding your creative expressions and responses.

Contemplation and Gratitude

Rest in this communion with God and express gratitude for his presence and artistic expression.

IMAGINATIVE CONTEMPLATION

Imagine yourself in the ancient world, standing in a bustling plaza of artisans. You see Bezalel, a craftsman whom God inspired in Exodus, his eyes alight with passion and creative purpose. He moves with a confidence and grace that speak of a higher calling, divine guidance.

His work is more than mere craftsmanship; it's a vivid display of divine artistry, a sacred dance between Creator and creation. You ponder deeply how this sacred calling manifests in your own life. In this moment of soul-stirring connection, you realize you are not a mere observer but a participant in this holy process. Reflect his glory through your expressions of creativity and art. As you work in the plaza, you become deeply aware of your role as a cocreator with the divine Artist, inspired to bring forth beauty and truth uniquely.

ECHOED VERSES

Hold (hands over heart):

Heavenly Father, your wisdom is my creative light.

Receive (hands open):

I am open to your divine guidance.

Hold (hands over heart):

Lord Christ, I find my true passion in your creativity.

Receive (hands open):

Fill me with your artistic spirit.

Hold (hands over heart):

Holy Spirit, through you, my talents flourish.

Receive (hands open):

I receive your gifts with gratitude.

SOULFUL BREATHING

Inhale deeply, embracing the Spirit of God, the same who imbued Bezalel with extraordinary skill and innovation. As you hold that breath, let your heart and mind savor the transcendent presence of the divine Artist within. Feel the warmth of his inspiration coursing through your veins, enlightening your soul with a celestial touch of creativity and wisdom.

As you exhale, allow faith in your God-given abilities to flow freely. With each breath, feel a deeper connection to the Creator, understanding that your artistry reflects his majesty.

Inhale: *God's Spirit fills me with creativity.*

Exhale: *I am skilled in his craft.*

Rest now in stillness, allowing today's Scripture passage to resonate within you, deepening your bond with the Creator and realizing his purpose for you.

SOULFUL REFLECTIONS

How does recognizing God's presence in your creative process transform your understanding of your talents and purpose?

How can you more fully surrender your artistic gifts to God, allowing his Spirit to guide your every brushstroke, word, or note?

CLOSING BENEDICTION

In the vast expanse of God's universe, you are an integral thread woven into its grand tapestry. May the Lord's blessings wrap around you as you embark on your journey and guide your heart in every creative pursuit. May his Spirit, rich in wisdom, skill, and understanding, fill your being, reminiscent of his anointing upon Bezalel. In each act of creativity, may you feel the divine Artist's presence seamlessly working through your spirit. Envision your life as a frame where you masterfully display God's boundless grace, overwhelming love, and sublime beauty in a sacred space. Let these divine attributes radiate through every brushstroke of your life, creating a masterpiece that reveals the glory of the Creator. In the holy name of Jesus, step forward with unyielding courage, ready to manifest the unique artistry that your Creator has lovingly instilled within you. Let your life's work be a testament to his magnificence, a beacon of his eternal light. Amen.

Service

Acting in Love and Humility

"If I then, your Lord and Teacher, have washed your feet, you also
ought to wash one another's feet. For I have given you an example,
that you also should do just as I have done to you."

JOHN 13:14–15

In the stillness, you find a hallowed space where your heart whispers
in cadence with the Divine. Here you discover a sacred alcove where
each breath carries a note of his eternal love. This stillness is not
merely an absence but a presence, the presence of the one you serve.

In the quiet, where God's voice is most sublime and most
apparent, you hear the soft echoes of divine whispers. You realize that
your every heartbeat is a testament to his abiding presence. The quiet
becomes a canvas painted with the colors of his grace and mercy,
inviting you to serve and act in love.

In the sacred, you stand on holy ground. Each moment becomes
a holy pause to shed the cloak of earthly concerns and be fully present
with your Creator. With him, the dance of divine love unfolds in the
depths of your heart. This sacred space is your meeting place to serve
the Father, Son, and Holy Spirit.

GUIDED MEDITATION

Focused Scriptural Meditation
Ponder John 13:14–15. Feel Jesus' gentle touch as he washes your feet, symbolizing humility and service.

Reflective Prayer and Listening
In thankfulness, connect with Jesus' boundless grace. Quietly pray, listening for his comforting voice.

Contemplation and Gratitude
As you consider Jesus washing your feet, rest in this sacred act, feeling cherished. Breathe in the peace that is present in this moment, offering thanks.

IMAGINATIVE CONTEMPLATION
In the dimness of the upper room, humility takes form. The Lord Christ, divinity robed in flesh, kneels before you. Gently, he cradles your travel-weary feet, washing away the dust. Each stroke of his hands is tender yet steadfast. Heavy with sacred silence, the air bears witness to this unspoken sermon and act of service.

You sit, your heart stirred. In this moment, the mundane transforms into the holy. Here the King of kings models the essence of the gospel, to love and serve others and to humble oneself. A deep truth resonates in the quiet room: true greatness in God's kingdom is found not in being served but in serving. This scene, a perfect expression of humility, invites your heart to journey deeper into the realm of selfless love and service.

ECHOED VERSES

Hold (hands over heart):

Heavenly Father, in love, I kneel before you.

Receive (hands open):

Teach me to kneel and serve in your name.

Hold (hands over heart):

Lord Christ, in your humility, you washed their feet.

Receive (hands open):

May I serve with the same love and grace.

Hold (hands over heart):

Holy Spirit, by your guidance, I become a servant.

Receive (hands open):

Let me reflect your servant's heart.

SOULFUL BREATHING

Inhale deeply, embracing the humility of Christ, your Lord and Teacher. Let his love fill your lungs, reminding you to serve others just as he loves you and washes your feet.

Exhale gently, releasing any pride or self-centeredness. As you breathe out, envision yourself extending Christ's humble service to those you meet, washing others' feet in selfless devotion.

Inhale: *As Christ washed my feet.*

Exhale: *I serve others in love.*

Rest in stillness, feeling God's love and humility in your heart. Accept the peace that comes with serving others, walking in the footsteps of Jesus.

SOULFUL REFLECTIONS

How can you embody Jesus' example of humility and service in your daily life and see each act of kindness as a reflection of his love?

In what ways does Jesus' act of washing the disciples' feet challenge your understanding of leadership and greatness in the kingdom of God?

CLOSING BENEDICTION

Go forth gently, embracing God's love and allowing his grace to guide you. As Jesus, your Lord and Teacher, demonstrated humility and service, so are you called to embody these virtues. May your hands become instruments of his peace, washing the feet of others in acts of love and humility. May the light of Christ illuminate your journey, guiding you in paths of compassion and kindness. Remember, in each act of service, small or grand, you echo the love of Jesus, who stooped to serve. May your heart be tuned to the whispers of the Holy Spirit, who leads you in wisdom and discernment. In the name of Jesus, may your life be a testament to his enduring love and grace. And now may the blessing of God Almighty—the Father, the Son, and the Holy Spirit—be upon you and remain with you always. Amen.

World

Interceding for Global Issues

I desire then that in every place the men should pray,
lifting holy hands without anger or quarreling.
1 TIMOTHY 2:8

In the stillness of your heart, where whispers outweigh words, there lies a space for prayer that is untouched by worldly strife. Here, in the gentle rhythm of your breathing, find the presence of the Divine. Raise your hands in reverence and lift your soul high above angry storms.

In the quiet of these moments, as the world fades into a hush, let your spirit listen for the echoes of God's love. This sacred calm, a canvas for the Creator's touch, invites you to paint your prayers with strokes of faith and hope and to understand the power of your now-peaceful heart.

In the sacred sanctuary of your inner being, where heaven and earth converge, feel the weight of global burdens lighten. As you intercede for the world, your prayers, like incense, rise and mingle with the Divine. Here, in this holy space, your intercessions become a bridge of grace to the Father, Son, and Holy Spirit.

GUIDED MEDITATION

Focused Scriptural Meditation

Reflect on 1 Timothy 2:8. Envision lifting holy hands, embracing peace and unity.

Reflective Prayer and Listening

Pray for global issues, seeking God's guidance. Listen for his words of hope, which cast aside discord.

Contemplation and Gratitude

Contemplate God's desire for harmony. Express gratitude for his guidance in interceding for the world.

IMAGINATIVE CONTEMPLATION

You see hands rising in unity toward a starry expanse under the dome of twilight. These are the hands of the faithful, which reach for the heavens in a silent act of prayer. Each with their own story of struggle and hope, the people join together in intercessory prayer.

Around you, the air is filled with a palpable sense of peace, as if the atmosphere resonates with the purity of their intentions. In this sacred assembly, quarreling dissolves into a harmony of souls, each heart beating in the rhythm of God's unwavering love.

In this moment, a weighty realization engulfs you. In God's presence, your differences fade, leaving only a shared humanity and a collective yearning for his love. This scene of divine communion echoes with a more reverential truth: in seeking the counsel of God, you find unity, and through his love, you find healing for your world.

ECHOED VERSES

Hold (hands over heart):

Holy Father, in your love, you gather the world's cries.

Receive (hands open):

We open our hearts to your boundless mercy, God.

Hold (hands over heart):

Lord Christ, you hear our prayers for peace and healing for the nations.

Receive (hands open):

In humility, we receive your guidance, trusting your wisdom.

Hold (hands over heart):

Holy Spirit, intercede to transform global despair into hope.

Receive (hands open):

Gratefully, we walk with your hope, renewing our world in love.

SOULFUL BREATHING

Inhale deeply, lifting your spirit like holy hands. Receive the sacred words *In every place, I should pray.* Feel their divine echo within, connecting you to a universal prayer.

Exhale slowly, releasing any anger, any quarreling. Let the phrase *lifting hands in peace* flow out, bringing peace to your soul. Surrender to this rhythm of grace and understanding.

Inhale: *In every place, I should pray.*

Exhale: *Lifting hands in peace.*

Rest in this stillness, allowing God's message to resonate in your heart. Know the peace of prayerful unity, feeling his presence in your calm spirit ever so deeply.

SOULFUL REFLECTIONS

How does lifting your hands in prayer symbolize surrender and trust in God's plan for the world? Reflect on the power that your prayers have to affect the global community.

In what ways can your prayer life become a transformative force not only in your walk with God but also in interceding for global issues and healing?

CLOSING BENEDICTION

May the Lord lead you safely when you're lost and keep you safe from harm. May he make your journey joyful with the amazing things he shows you. May he bring you back home. In the name of Jesus, who calms our fears and soothes our anxieties, may your heart find rest. As you intercede for the world, may your prayers rise like incense, a pleasing aroma to the Lord. May your hands, lifted in prayer, be strengthened for service, tender in touch, and generous in giving. And may your journey through this day bring you closer to God's heart, where you find true joy. In Christ's name, may God's grace, mercy, and peace be with you. Amen.

DAY 28

Family

Praying with Loved Ones

"As for me and my house,
we will serve the LORD."
JOSHUA 24:15

In the stillness, you find yourself at a crossroads. Whispers of the present and echoes of ancient prayers vie for your heart. In this serene place, consider your path of devotion, unwavering like a river. It relentlessly journeys toward a divine horizon, a testament to inherited faith.

In the quiet, the gentle murmur of your home's heartbeat beckons. Here, among the walls that witness your life, lies sacred ground. As you gather with loved ones, hands clasped in prayer, feel the shared warmth of faith, a silent symphony of unity, an invisible yet palpable bond, drawing each heart nearer to God.

In the sacred space of shared belief, your family stands together, interwoven with threads of devotion. Your collective resolve strengthens in each whispered prayer and in every shared Scripture reading. Like a steadfast lighthouse against the storm, your household's declaration stands firm: as for us, we will serve the Father, Son, and Holy Spirit.

GUIDED MEDITATION

Focused Scriptural Meditation

Contemplate Joshua 24:15. Imagine your family, united in faith, declaring you will serve the Lord.

Reflective Prayer and Listening

Pray for your loved ones. Ask God to guide your family, making your home a place of steadfast faith.

Contemplation and Gratitude

Ponder the blessing of your God-centered family. Express gratitude for ancestral love.

IMAGINATIVE CONTEMPLATION

In the hush of dusk, Joshua stands with his family. The setting sun casts a holy light, illuminating their earnest faces. He speaks, "As for me and my house, we will serve the LORD." These words, simple yet inspirational, ripple through the hearts of his loved ones. The whisper of wind through the trees echoes Joshua's declaration, a sacred chorus affirming their collective pledge.

This moment, transcending time, speaks of a deep commitment beyond words. Now see the faces of your own family. Together you stand as you make with the Lord a covenant not just of duty but of love and shared faith. Here, in the unity of family and presence of the Lord, lies the essence of genuine service—a service that is born not of obligation but of a heartfelt desire to walk in his ways.

ECHOED VERSES

Hold (hands over heart):

Heavenly Father, in your steadfast love, you guide our family's steps.

Receive (hands open):

We follow you, trusting in your wisdom and grace.

Hold (hands over heart):

Lord Christ, your strength upholds us in times of trial and joy.

Receive (hands open):

In this strength, we find peace and unyielding courage.

Hold (hands over heart):

Holy Spirit, intercede and illuminate our path, clear and true.

Receive (hands open):

Guided by this light, we walk confidently in faith.

SOULFUL BREATHING

As you breathe deeply, let the words *as for me and my house* fill your lungs. Imagine your family united in serving the Lord, drawing closer with every breath.

With each exhale, release the phrase *We will serve the Lord*. Feel the commitment and love flowing out, touching every part of your life with divine purpose.

Inhale: *As for me and my house.*

Exhale: *We will serve the Lord.*

Let the essence of service and family devotion linger in your heart in this moment of stillness. Embrace the peace that comes from a life dedicated to God's path.

SOULFUL REFLECTIONS

How can you foster a home environment that mirrors Joshua's commitment to serving the Lord and nurtures faith in every interaction?

Reflect on the choices you make daily. In what ways can these choices reflect a commitment to God, influencing your family's spiritual journey?

CLOSING BENEDICTION

May the grace of our Lord Jesus Christ enfold you, beloved, as you walk in his ways. In your dwelling, may peace and unity in Christ flourish, mirroring the steadfast love of our Savior. As you gather with family, may your prayers rise like incense, a pleasing aroma to the Lord. May his wisdom guide your conversations, his patience temper your interactions, and his joy strengthen your heart. In times of challenge or doubt, remember that you are not alone, for God is faithful. Cling to his unfailing promises. May your home be a haven of grace, where forgiveness echoes the heart of Jesus and love is the language spoken. And now may the Lord bless and keep you; may his face shine upon you and be gracious to you. May he lift his countenance upon you, granting peace in the name of Jesus. Amen.

Overcome

Addressing Obstacles Head-On

He said to me, "My grace is sufficient for you,
for my power is made perfect in weakness."
2 CORINTHIANS 12:9

In the stillness, you hear a whisper that echoes through the chambers of your soul. It's a gentle yet powerful reminder: his grace is enough. When the world blurs in turmoil, his voice is the calm that steadies your heart in your weakest moments, anchoring you in divine peace.

In the quiet, your struggles seem amplified, painting shadows of doubt across your journey. Yet it is here, in the peaceful moments of introspection, where his power manifests most clearly. Rather than diminishing your spirit, your vulnerabilities become the base for his strength, illustrating the perfect harmony of your dependence on him.

In the sacred, there lies a truth as old as time yet as fresh as morning dew: his grace is sufficient. It's in these sacred pauses of life that you feel his presence most intimately. These pauses become a sanctuary where holy power is perfected in your weakness and transforms obstacles into stepping stones toward a deeper faith in the Father, Son, and Holy Spirit.

GUIDED MEDITATION

Focused Scriptural Meditation

Read 2 Corinthians 12:9 and remember his grace is enough. His power is perfect in your weakness.

Reflective Prayer and Listening

Talk to God about your obstacles and openly share your feelings. Listen for assurance of his strength.

Contemplation and Gratitude

Contemplate God's sufficient grace and give thanks for his strength in your life during times of struggle.

IMAGINATIVE CONTEMPLATION

In a quiet room, you see a solitary figure kneeling, burdened yet hopeful. Ancient prayers softly echo off the walls. Outside, the world sleeps, oblivious to the sacred struggle within.

The figure's voice is fragile yet rises in a heartfelt plea for strength. The air becomes charged with a holy presence. A celestial light casts a soft glow over the weary face. In this intimate communion, a divine whisper caresses the soul: "My grace is sufficient for you."

Here in this sacred moment, frailty becomes a vessel for God's power. Tears of struggle transform into tears of surrender, each a testament to the compelling exchange of human weakness for divine strength. Once a place of solitude, the room now resonates with the truth of divine sufficiency, offering a sanctuary of peace to all who ask.

ECHOED VERSES

Hold (hands over heart):

Heavenly Father, your grace is sufficient in my weakness.

Receive (hands open):

In your strength, I find peace.

Hold (hands over heart):

Lord Christ, you achieve power in my frailties.

Receive (hands open):

In humility, I receive your might.

Hold (hands over heart):

Holy Spirit, your wisdom and intercession overcome obstacles.

Receive (hands open):

I triumph in you.

SOULFUL BREATHING

Aim to align your breath with the comforting message of 2 Corinthians, deepening your inner peace and spiritual connection with God. Inhale deeply, drawing in God's grace. Let his words *My grace is sufficient* fill your being, affirming his power in your weakness and nurturing your soul.

Exhale slowly, releasing obstacles and fears. Think, *My weakness is your power*, feeling his strength in your vulnerability and embracing peace and surrender with each breath you release.

Inhale: *Your grace is sufficient.*

Exhale: *My weakness is your power.*

Rest in stillness, absorbing the enlightening truth that God's power is perfected in our weakness. Comprehend this divine peace, feeling connected and grounded in his unending love.

SOULFUL REFLECTIONS

In your moments of weakness, how do you experience God's grace transforming your limitations into strengths and reflecting his perfect power in your life's journey?

How does acknowledging your vulnerabilities before God lead you to a deeper reliance on his strength, and in what ways has this reshaped your understanding of divine providence?

CLOSING BENEDICTION

May the Lord bless and keep you; his grace is your shield and strength. In every trial, let his promise echo in your heart: his grace is sufficient, and his power is perfected in weakness. Remember that in times of doubt, he is your steadfast companion; his mighty hand navigates you through each challenge. May the peace of God, which surpasses all understanding, guard your heart and mind in Christ Jesus. When uncertainty clouds your path, hold fast to his unchanging faithfulness. Let his light guide your steps. His wisdom illuminates your journey. In the name of Jesus, face each day with courage and hope. Know the Almighty is with you, transforming obstacles into opportunities for his glory. Trust in his providential care, embracing the fullness of his blessings. Now go forth in his strength, living a life that reflects the Lord's endless love and grace. Amen.

Prophecy

Declaring God's Truth

"Your sons and your daughters shall prophesy,
your old men shall dream dreams,
and your young men shall see visions."
JOEL 2:28

In the stillness, you find not a whisper of this world but a gentle, holy murmur in the depths of your soul. God's voice, soft yet unmistakable, calls to you. Like a delicate breeze, it brushes against your heart, whispering of divine truth and wisdom.

In the quiet, the outcry of life fades, leaving a hallowed space where prophecy takes root. Here, in this sacred silence, your heart listens for the echo of ancient words: "Your sons and your daughters shall prophesy." These words, timeless and true, invite you to envision a future filled with the marvels God has revealed to us.

In the sacred, dreams and visions find their genesis. The old dream dreams rich with wisdom; the young see visions vibrant with hope's hue. In this holy communion, you stand at the crossroads of time and eternity, witnessing the prophetic promise that calls all to declare the enduring truth of the Father, Son, and Holy Spirit.

GUIDED MEDITATION

Focused Scriptural Meditation

Reflect on Joel 2:28, for you are a part of this prophecy. God's prophetic truth unfolds in your life.

Reflective Prayer and Listening

Ask God to awaken his gifts in you. Seek his wisdom for how to understand and declare his truth.

Contemplation and Gratitude

In quiet gratitude, acknowledge God's promise. Thank him for the gift of being a vessel of his divine words.

IMAGINATIVE CONTEMPLATION

Imagine an ancient, knotted oak standing sentinel under a starry sky. Around it gather souls old and young. A young person steps forward and speaks. The resonant voice cuts through the silence, declaring visions of a future woven by God's wise hands. The words wash over the listeners, engraving on their hearts images of restoration.

Imagine an elderly person, hair silver as the moon, whispering of dreams in which angels tread. The veil between heaven and earth is thin in these musings, revealing glimpses of God's majesty. The gentle words float, carrying a message of enduring hope.

In this sacred gathering, prophecies and dreams merge, creating a foundation of divine wisdom and hope. This moment calls the soul to a deeper understanding of God's mysterious ways, nurturing an intimate communion.

ECHOED VERSES

Hold (hands over heart):

Heavenly Father, your whispers shape futures and dreams unseen.

Receive (hands open):

I listen, heart open, embracing your divine prophecy.

Hold (hands over heart):

Lord Christ, by your grace I shall prophesy, dream dreams, and see visions.

Receive (hands open):

In awe, I receive, eyes wide to your revelations.

Hold (hands over heart):

Holy Spirit, your guiding words weave a tapestry of holy truths.

Receive (hands open):

I hold your promises, treasuring each sacred word.

SOULFUL BREATHING

As you breathe in, envision sons and daughters prophesying. Your breath carries visions of the old dreaming and the young seeing. Inhale the divine promise, feeling God's truth awaken within.

Each time you breathe out, release doubt. Let visions and dreams, prophesied words, flow from you. Surrender to God's plan and encounter a deeply felt calm as you immerse yourself in his eternal truth.

Inhale: *Sons and daughters shall prophesy.*

Exhale: *Dreams arise, and visions are seen.*

In stillness, hear God's prophetic words. Let your heart hold dreams and visions, feeling his peace. Find a deep connection with the Divine's eternal promise in this sacred silence.

SOULFUL REFLECTIONS

How does the prophecy in Joel 2:28, where God promises to pour out his Spirit, inspire you to seek a deeper, more personal connection with the Holy Spirit in your daily life?

Consider how God might speak to you uniquely when you reflect on the dreams and visions he promised in Joel 2:28. How can you be more open to receiving and understanding his guidance?

CLOSING BENEDICTION

In the grace of our Lord Jesus Christ, may your heart be tuned to the whispers of prophecy echoing while you pray. In light of the ancient words of Joel, may your life manifest the richness of God's truths. May you be encouraged by the Spirit, prophesy with courage, and speak life into the dry bones of this world. May you dream dreams that stir the waters of complacency and call for transformation. May visions as bright as morning light guide your steps on paths of righteousness. As a vessel of divine expression, may your voice declare the love of God. Now walk in humility and strength as the echoes of these heavenly declarations mark your journey. In the name of Jesus, be blessed, be empowered, and illuminate his eternal truth. Amen.

Healing

Praying for Well-Being

The prayer of faith will save the one who is sick,
and the Lord will raise him up.
JAMES 5:15

In the stillness, your heart whispers a prayer, a melody of hope amid the turmoil of life. Like a gentle stream, faith flows, serene and steadfast. Here, in the hush of God's presence, healing begins. Each breath is a silent petition; each pause a space for grace. In this sacred stillness, you find strength one prayerful moment at a time.

In the quiet, your soul finds refuge, a sanctuary where whispers of divine love echo. This is where prayer transforms from mere words to a dance of trust, twirling in the arms of the Almighty. In these moments of tranquility, the peace that surpasses all understanding replaces your worries, cradling you in celestial calmness.

In the sacred pause of prayer, you connect to the source of all well-being. In the hallowed space where heaven touches earth, your faith intertwines with God's promises. The prayer of faith resounds, a symphony of hope and restoration. Here healing transcends the physical, foreshadowing an eternity with the Father, Son, and Holy Spirit.

GUIDED MEDITATION

Focused Scriptural Meditation

Contemplate James 5:15 as you imagine faith's power in healing and well-being. Let these words resonate within you.

Reflective Prayer and Listening

Pray for healing for yourself and for others. Trust in God's promise. Listen for his comforting response.

Contemplation and Gratitude

Reflect on God's healing presence. Thank him for his unfailing love and care.

IMAGINATIVE CONTEMPLATION

You see believers gathered around a hospital bed in a humble room, interlocking their hands in prayer. The air is heavy with faith as whispers of hope rise like incense over a sick friend. You watch as the patient, wrapped in the warmth of prayer, begins to feel a divine presence enfolding their body and soul. The eyes of the faithful who have gathered together, once closed in devotion, now shine with an unspoken understanding of God's power.

The collective prayer uplifts and comforts the patient's spirit. It's a living testament to the promise of today's verse: the Lord will raise those who have faith and will receive prayers. In this act of communal prayer, everyone present—you included—experiences a deeper connection with the Divine, affirming the substantial impact of faith and the power of God's love.

ECHOED VERSES

Hold (hands over heart):

Heavenly Father, your touch brings healing and strength to the weary.

Receive (hands open):

I open my heart to your restorative grace.

Hold (hands over heart):

Lord Christ, in your love, comfort those who are burdened and broken.

Receive (hands open):

I receive your peace, which surpasses understanding.

Hold (hands over heart):

Holy Spirit, your presence mends the crushed and brokenhearted.

Receive (hands open):

In faith, I welcome your wholeness and renewal.

SOULFUL BREATHING

Inhale deeply, feeling the faith-filled promise of healing from James 5:15. Let the phrase *A prayer of faith saves* envelop you as, with each breath, you draw in hope and divine restoration.

Exhale slowly, releasing doubts as you ask the Lord to raise up those who are hurting and in need of God's healing. Feel the comforting assurance of God's presence and the peaceful release of his healing power. Let the Holy Spirit guide your prayers toward sick and brokenhearted people. Whisper their names.

Inhale: *A prayer of faith saves.*

Exhale: *Lord, raise up [say names here].*

In stillness, cherish the tranquility of God's promise. Let the power of his healing love and faith resonate within you, nurturing a deep, enduring peace in your heart.

SOULFUL REFLECTIONS

How does your understanding of God's healing power in James 5:15 shape how you approach life's challenges and deepen your faith?

Reflect on a time when you felt God's presence during a trial. How did this experience change your perception of his promised love and care?

CLOSING BENEDICTION

May you find solace in the arms of the Almighty, who weaves healing into the essence of your being. May his peace cast aside the challenges that burden your spirit and envelop you like a gentle mist. Let faith be the anchor that steadies your heart, and may you know that in his presence, restoration is more than a distant hope; it is a present reality. As you walk through valleys shadowed by pain, may you feel the warmth of his unending love, a light guiding you toward renewal. Let every prayer whispered in the quiet corners of your soul be a testament to his unwavering faithfulness. He knows you, hears and cherishes you, and tirelessly works for your well-being. May you hear his tender whisper in the sacred stillness, assuring you that you are never alone. Now see his healing hands extended toward you, offering strength and comfort. In Jesus' name. Amen.

Miracles

Believing in God's Power

"I tell you, whatever you ask in prayer,
believe that you have received it, and it will be yours."
MARK 11:24

In the stillness, you discover a whisper, a gentle murmur echoing through the chambers of your soul. It speaks of miracles, a faith untamed by the world's discord. In these still moments, as you sit nestled in God's presence, the truth of Mark 11:24 emerges like a star in the twilight sky: prayer demonstrates your belief that God's power brings miracles into being.

In the quiet, there's a sacred dance of hope and patience. Each prayer offered at the altar of faith carries the fragrance of trust in God's promises. Your faith is not just spoken; it's a song you whisper in reverence, confident in miracles yet to be revealed.

In the sacred, your soul learns the art of waiting, of trusting in the unseen tapestry woven by God's all-knowing hand. This holy sanctuary becomes a cradle for miracles, for each whispered prayer held by the Divine. And in this consecrated place, you receive the miracles that bloom from the Father, Son, and Holy Spirit.

GUIDED MEDITATION

Focused Scriptural Meditation

Contemplate Mark 11:24 and believe the promise of asking and receiving as you lay your burdens before God.

Reflective Prayer and Listening

Share your desires with God in heartfelt petition, believing he hears and acts. Listen for his affirming peace.

Contemplation and Gratitude

In gratitude, recognize God's miraculous ability. Thank him for his faithfulness and unfailing love.

IMAGINATIVE CONTEMPLATION

Imagine the hush of a golden morning, where sunlight caresses olive trees in a biblical garden. You find yourself in ancient Jerusalem. The air is thick with whispers of miracles and the power of unwavering faith. You see Jesus, his gaze piercing yet tender amid the bustling crowd. Like a gentle stream, his words wash over your soul: "Whatever you ask in prayer, believe that you have received it, and it will be yours."

His voice resonates to the very core of your being. You close your eyes, envisioning your deepest prayers. In your heart's garden, these seeds of faith sprout, nurtured by trust in his promise.

This moment transcends time, urging you to grasp the true essence of belief. It's not just about seeing but about envisioning with eyes of faith, where the unseen becomes tangible and the impossible possible.

ECHOED VERSES

Hold (hands over heart):

    Heavenly Father, I find strength and comfort in your presence.

Receive (hands open):

    Your grace flows, filling me with peace and hope.

Hold (hands over heart):

    Lord Christ, you deeply understand my struggles and fears.

Receive (hands open):

    In your love, I am understood and cherished.

Hold (hands over heart):

    Holy Spirit, guide me in truth and wisdom.

Receive (hands open):

    Your guidance illuminates my path, bringing clarity.

SOULFUL BREATHING

As you breathe in deeply, receive the words of Mark 11:24: "Whatever you ask in prayer, believe." Let each inhale deepen your faith as God's promise of miracles fills you.

With each exhale, release doubt, whispering, *Receive with a believing heart.* Let go of uncertainties, feeling God's assurance flow through you and aligning your spirit with his unending power. Exhale your most soulful prayers as seeds of faith sprout and are nurtured by trust in his promises.

Inhale: *Ask in faithful prayer.*

Exhale: *Receive with a believing heart.*

In stillness, reflect on God's Word. Your heart, calm and assured, understands the depth of his promise. In your soul, peace and faith intertwine, grounding you in divine love.

SOULFUL REFLECTIONS

How does your faith in God's power to perform miracles shape your daily life and influence your choices, reactions, and trust in his plans for your future?

Reflect on a time when you felt distant from God's presence. How can embracing his promise in Mark 11:24 guide you back to a deeper, more trusting relationship with him?

CLOSING BENEDICTION

May you find strength in the grace and peace of our Lord Jesus Christ. As you journey through trials and joys, remember his promise in Mark 11, to pray with faith and believe that God will answer your prayers. May your faith be a beacon, guiding you through darkness to his eternal light. Let his wisdom be your compass and his Word your map as you navigate life's trials. In your moments of doubt, may his Spirit whisper truths to your heart, reaffirming your place in his grand design. May your days be filled with the joy of his presence, the comfort of his love, and the courage of his Spirit. As you walk in his footsteps, may you embody his grace, extend his forgiveness, and radiate his love in the name of Jesus. Amen.

Petition

Never Stop Asking

"I tell you, ask, and it will be given to you;
seek, and you will find;
knock, and it will be opened to you.
For everyone who asks receives,
and the one who seeks finds,
and to the one who knocks it will be opened."

LUKE 11:9–10

In the stillness, there's a whisper, soft as the flutter of a dove's wing yet potent in its presence. The world's racket fades in this peaceful solitude, and a heavenly voice becomes clear. You find yourself at the threshold of communion, where each heartbeat longs to petition God.

In the quiet, there's a truth waiting to unfold. In these moments, away from the world's relentless roar, you discover the essence of prayer—a conversation beyond words, a seeking beyond sight, a place where your soul speaks and listens in equal measure.

In the sacred, there's an invitation to journey to the deep wells of faith, where doubts dissolve. Today's verses whisper an age-old promise. Each earnest petition, each sincere seeking, each persistent knock opens a door, revealing paths to grace and moments of divine encounters with the Father, Son, and Holy Spirit.

GUIDED MEDITATION

Focused Scriptural Meditation

Reflect on Luke 11:9–10 and let the promise of receiving, finding, and opening resonate within you.

Reflective Prayer and Listening

Open your soul and present your requests to God. Listen for his guidance and trust in his promise to answer.

Contemplation and Gratitude

In gratitude, acknowledge God's faithfulness in responding to your petitions. Rest in his assurance.

IMAGINATIVE CONTEMPLATION

In the hush of dawn, you find yourself standing before an ancient door. The wood, worn by time, whispers tales of countless seekers who have stood where you now stand. Your heart is full of both hope and hesitation.

You raise your hand, feeling the weight of your need, the depth of your desire. The knock that resounds from your knuckles echoes on the door and within your soul. It's a rhythmic plea of persistence and faith.

The air is thick with expectancy in this sacred pause. Your ears, sensitive to the slightest shift, hear a turning from within, the sound of movement, the answering stir of the Divine. It is a hallowed moment, an intimate dance where heaven leans close. You wait, knowing the door will open, for everyone who asks receives. The promise stands unbroken.

ECHOED VERSES

Hold (hands over heart):

Heavenly Father, you listen when I call, and you understand my deepest needs.

Receive (hands open):

By your grace, I receive answers, abundant and true.

Hold (hands over heart):

Lord Christ, in your wisdom, guide my steps, leading me forward.

Receive (hands open):

Your guidance brings clarity and reveals paths of peace.

Hold (hands over heart):

Holy Spirit, your guiding hand sustains me, even through my darkest hours.

Receive (hands open):

In love, I find strength endlessly flowing from you.

SOULFUL BREATHING

Inhale deeply, drawing in the promise of today's verses: *Ask, and it will be given.* Let these words fill you, expanding your faith and heart with each breath.

Exhale slowly, releasing doubts. *Seek, and you will find.* Resonate with these words, letting go of worries. Feel a penetrating spiritual calm and connection with each outward breath.

Inhale: *Ask, and it will be given.*

Exhale: *Seek, and you will find.*

Rest in stillness now, embracing the peace of God's promise. Let your heart be anchored in his words, feeling an ever-deepening inner tranquility. Wait, knowing the door will open. You have asked by faith, and you will receive in God's way, in his time, and according to his will. The promise stands unbroken.

SOULFUL REFLECTIONS

How does your persistent prayer reflect your trust in God's timing and plans, and how can this perseverance deepen your understanding of his character and his desires for your life?

In what ways can your continuous seeking of God's presence and guidance shape your daily choices and actions, leading you toward a life that genuinely embodies his love and purpose for you?

CLOSING BENEDICTION

May the grace of our Lord Jesus Christ hold you, the love of God surround you, and the fellowship of the Holy Spirit guide you. As you have asked in faith, so trust that God hears your petitions. In your seeking, may your heart be enlightened; in your knocking, may doors of opportunity and understanding be opened to you. Remember that in his mercy, the Lord accommodates the voice of your supplications. May your journey be graced with the assurance that in every moment that you ask, seek, and knock, your heavenly Father listens with a heart of infinite compassion and wisdom. Walk in the confidence of God's unchanging promises, and may his peace, which surpasses all understanding, guard your heart and mind in the name of Jesus. Amen.

Joy

Celebrating God's Faithfulness

Enter his gates with thanksgiving,
and his courts with praise!
Give thanks to him; bless his name!
PSALM 100:4

In the stillness, you find a whispered invitation, a gentle call to draw nearer to the heart of the Divine. Within this calm serenity, your soul can truly listen, hearing the echoes of ancient delight and joy that resonate through time. This stillness is a holy space where God's unchanging love becomes a tangible presence in your life.

In the quiet, a captivating beauty blossoms like dawn's first light. Here, in the murmur of your heart, you sense an abundant and enchanting truth. The quiet is not an emptiness but a canvas for God's grace, where each stroke of his love paints a masterpiece of joy within you.

In the sacred, you stand on holy ground where joy and reverence intertwine, creating a stage for praise. Joy flows freely from your spirit and produces a light that cascades into God's eternal courts. It is here, at this divine crossroads, where your soul dances a delightful dance of heavenly pleasure and bliss in the presence of the Father, Son, and Holy Spirit.

GUIDED MEDITATION

Focused Scriptural Meditation

Reflect on Psalm 100:4 and feel the joy of entering the Lord's presence with thanksgiving and praise.

Reflective Prayer and Listening

In this time of sacred communion, talk to God about his faithfulness. Share your joy. Listen for his voice and affirm his steadfast love.

Contemplation and Gratitude

In silence, cherish his faithfulness. Express gratitude, carrying this joy throughout your day.

IMAGINATIVE CONTEMPLATION

As you approach a set of gates, your heart swells with joy. The gates before you are not hewn of iron or wood but of thanksgiving, their hinges oiled by gratitude. Each step you take resonates with the rhythm of your thankful spirit.

As you enter God's courts, a symphony of praise wraps around you, the air abuzz with countless voices lifted in adoration. Your soul dances to this melody of praise. Like rising incense, each note is a testimony to his enduring faithfulness.

In this sacred space, you find yourself whispering words of blessing as your spirit is humbled and exalted. Giving thanks transforms you, drawing you closer to the heart of God. In this moment, you understand that joy is more than an emotion; it is a sacred communion, a dance with the Divine, an eternal echo of his faithfulness.

ECHOED VERSES

Hold (hands over heart):

Holy Father, you are faithful in every season of life.

Receive (hands open):

I receive your constant love and feel deeply grateful.

Hold (hands over heart):

Lord Christ, your grace sustains me through each moment's need.

Receive (hands open):

In your mercy, I find strength and renewed hope.

Hold (hands over heart):

Holy Spirit, your guidance is a lamp to my path.

Receive (hands open):

I receive your wisdom and walk in light and joy.

SOULFUL BREATHING

As you inhale deeply, hear the words *I enter your gates joyfully*. Let gratitude fill your lungs as you reflect on God's faithfulness and joy. Feel his presence in every breath as you enter his gates with thanksgiving and his courts with praise.

Exhale gently, whispering, *Echo with my praise*. Release any burdens, allowing your praise and joy to flow freely. With each exhale, acknowledge the Lord's greatness and feel a deeper, more joyful connection to his eternal grace.

Inhale: *I enter your gates joyfully.*

Exhale: *Echo with my praise.*

In stillness, encounter the serenity, letting the truth of today's verse resonate. Feel God's faithfulness and love enriching your soul, offering peace and a rich connection to your Creator.

SOULFUL REFLECTIONS

When have you felt the most joyful in God's presence, and how can you incorporate that sense of divine joy into your daily life?

In what ways does your praise reflect the steadfast nature of God's love, and how does this shape your understanding of gratitude?

CLOSING BENEDICTION

May the joy of the Lord be your strength as you enter his gates with thanksgiving and his courts with praise. May your heart always sing of his endless love and faithfulness, for his mercy endures forever. Let gratitude illuminate your path every moment, for the Almighty knows and cherishes you. As you journey forward, may the peace of Christ, which surpasses all understanding, embrace you. May his unceasing grace mark your days, and may you rest at night in the assurance of his watchful care. Remember that he is your refuge in every trial, an ever-present help in times of trouble. May his wisdom guide you, his power uphold you, and his love comfort you. In the name of Jesus, go forth in his joy, radiating his light and love to all you encounter. Amen.

Discern

Seeking God's Wisdom

Trust in the LORD with all your heart,
and do not lean on your own understanding.
In all your ways acknowledge him,
and he will make straight your paths.
PROVERBS 3:5–6

In the stillness, you feel a whispering wind that speaks of a trust deeper than the roots of an ancient tree. You stand at the threshold of divine wisdom in this sacred hush, where the world's noise fades. Here your heart learns to release the heavy burdens of self-reliance, opening to the gentle refuge of God's understanding.

In the quiet, you discover a peaceful river flowing gently through the landscapes of your soul. This tranquil stream carries away the debris of doubt and confusion, leaving behind the clear waters of God's wisdom. As your feet wade into these serene shallows, the clarity of his guidance surpasses your understanding.

In the sacred space of surrender, you encounter the unfolding of his perfect plan. In the temple of your heart, you allow his hand to guide your steps. Each step in this divine dance of trust becomes a testament to the unfailing love and direction of the Father, Son, and Holy Spirit.

GUIDED MEDITATION

Focused Scriptural Meditation

Consider Proverbs 3:5–6 as you place your trust entirely in the Lord. His wisdom far surpasses yours.

Reflective Prayer and Listening

Pray, seek, and listen for his voice as he affirms your trust in his understanding, not your own.

Contemplation and Gratitude

Reflect on God's faithfulness. Express gratitude for his promise to direct your paths. Accept his peace.

IMAGINATIVE CONTEMPLATION

Imagine yourself wandering in a flourishing garden, your heart full of questions, your mind a whirlwind of thoughts. The path before you twists and turns, obscured by the overgrowth of your uncertainties. As you stumble, you hear a whisper: *Take my hand. Trust in me with all your heart and do not lean on your understanding.*

Feel your burdens lighten with each step. Feel your hand slip into the hand of Christ as you navigate his path. You realize that this path is not a journey of solitude. In the truth of his creation, you pledge to acknowledge him in all your ways. A transformative tranquility wraps around you. In this moment of divine clarity, you understand that he is making your paths straight, guiding you toward a horizon filled with his grace and truth.

ECHOED VERSES

Hold (hands over heart):

Heavenly Father, you lead, and I follow. Your ways, not mine.

Receive (hands open):

I open my heart, receiving your divine guidance.

Hold (hands over heart):

Lord Christ, you light my path. In you I trust.

Receive (hands open):

Your guidance flows freely to me in your love.

Hold (hands over heart):

Holy Spirit, you speak, and I listen. Your whispers are my compass.

Receive (hands open):

I ask for your wisdom. It fills my soul.

SOULFUL BREATHING

Inhale deeply, embracing confidence in the Lord, and whisper, *Trust in the Lord*. Let his wisdom fill your lungs, your heart. With each breath, acknowledge him, absorbing his guidance. Feel your path become straighter and more evident—the path of his choosing, not yours.

Exhale slowly, releasing your own understanding. Silently breathe out, *He will guide me*. Let go of doubts and fears. As you breathe out, feel his presence, his peace. Surrender all your ways and find calm in his assurance.

Inhale: *Trust in the Lord.*

Exhale: *He will guide me.*

Rest in this stillness, allowing God's words to resonate within. In this quiet, find strength in trust and guidance in surrender. Desire his peace, feeling deeply connected and divinely guided.

SOULFUL REFLECTIONS

In what ways have you experienced God's guidance in your life, and how can reflecting on these moments deepen your trust in his plans for your future?

How do your daily choices and actions reflect your trust in God, and in what areas of your life do you need his wisdom to help you align more closely with his will?

CLOSING BENEDICTION

May the peace of the Lord Christ go with you wherever he may send you. May he guide you through the wilderness and overgrown paths and protect you through the storms. May he bring you home rejoicing at the wonders he has shown you and rejoicing in the name of Jesus Christ, who reigns eternally with the Father and the Holy Spirit. May the blessing of God Almighty—the Father, the Son, and the Holy Spirit—be upon you and remain with you always. Trust in the Lord with all your heart; lean not on your own understanding. In all your ways acknowledge him, and he shall direct your paths. Go forth in peace to love and serve the Lord. Amen.

Covenant

Promising Heartfelt Devotion

All the paths of the LORD are steadfast love and faithfulness,
for those who keep his covenant and his testimonies.
PSALM 25:10

In the stillness, you hear a whisper of God's unwavering covenant, a soft murmur that resonates within your heart. Here, in the hush away from life's commotion, his steadfast faithfulness unfurls, illuminating your path. This gentle yet pivotal divine assurance cradles your spirit in an eternal agreement.

In the quiet, your soul becomes a fertile ground for reflection, a place where the seeds of his Word take root. Each verse, a beacon of his covenant with you, blooms. In these moments, God's testimonies resonate, echoing through your very being and reminding you of the enduring strength of heartfelt devotion and his eternal pledge.

In the sacred, in a tranquil sanctuary, you meet God's presence. His truths become vividly apparent in this hallowed stillness, filling your life with his grace and mercy. Here you understand the essence of his covenant, an unbreakable bond of love and faithfulness that surrounds you with the grace and everlasting peace of the Father, Son, and Holy Spirit.

GUIDED MEDITATION

Focused Scriptural Meditation

Reflect on Psalm 25:10 and contemplate how God's paths embody love and faithfulness in your life.

Reflective Prayer and Listening

In seeking divine guidance, express your commitment to God's covenant. Listen for his guidance and feel his steadfast faithfulness encircle you.

Contemplation and Gratitude

In silent gratitude, cherish God's unchanging love and truth, letting his faithfulness strengthen your heart.

IMAGINATIVE CONTEMPLATION

In the hush of dawn, you wander down a lush path, where the morning mist whispers God's promises. The walk winds through an ancient forest, each tree a sentinel of God's unwavering faithfulness. In this sacred space, amid the beauty of God's creation, you realize that keeping his covenant is not a burdensome task but an act of heartfelt devotion.

This moment, wrapped in the serenity of nature, becomes a sanctuary for contemplation. You ponder the spiritual significance of this journey, realizing it's not just about following his testimonies but about living them. Here you understand that this journey is about reaching a destination and cherishing the steps you take toward it. In the forest's quiet, your heart whispers a promise to keep his covenant, the unbreakable, infinite grace that binds you to him forever.

ECHOED VERSES

Hold (hands over heart):

Heavenly Father, you guide me in truth and love.

Receive (hands open):

I know your guidance and feel your presence.

Hold (hands over heart):

Lord Christ, your promises are my strength and hope.

Receive (hands open):

In your promises, I find courage and peace.

Hold (hands over heart):

Holy Spirit, your comfort fills my weary soul.

Receive (hands open):

Filled by your comfort, I am renewed and whole.

SOULFUL BREATHING

Inhale deeply, drawing in the steadfast love of the Lord. Feel his faithfulness fill your being as you welcome his covenant. With each breath, internalize his unwavering devotion and truth. Inhale his promise that he remains unchanged, always issuing a boundless wellspring of grace and eternally knitting your soul to his.

Exhale slowly, releasing doubts and feeling the Lord's steadfast love and faithfulness flow through you. As you breathe out, reflect on his promises and feel a reformative sense of calm and connection to him in your spirit.

Inhale: *Your path is love.*

Exhale: *Your promise is eternal.*

Rest in stillness, letting today's verse from Psalms resonate in your heart. Know the peace and understanding that come from a deeper relationship with God and feel his loving presence within and around you.

SOULFUL REFLECTIONS

In what ways do you experience God's steadfast love in your daily walk, and how can reflecting on his faithfulness deepen your commitment to living out his covenant in your life?

How do God's promises influence how you approach challenges and decisions and how you align your actions with his divine will?

CLOSING BENEDICTION

May the Lord bless you and keep you as you walk in the light of his steadfast love. May your heart turn to his whispers as they guide you along paths of righteousness for his name's sake. Remember, his faithfulness endures forever for those who keep his covenant and bear his testimonies in their lives. May your steps be firm, anchored in his truth, and your spirit uplifted by the assurance of his presence. In moments of trial, may you find solace in his unwavering grace, and in times of joy, may your praises echo the depths of your gratitude. May the peace of Christ reign in your heart, a peace that surpasses all understanding, guarding your mind and soul in him. And as you journey onward, may you be a beacon of his love and light to those around you. In the name of Jesus. Amen.

Gifts

Seeking Spiritual Endowments

There are varieties of gifts, but the same Spirit; and there are varieties of service, but the same Lord; and there are varieties of activities, but it is the same God who empowers them all in everyone.

1 CORINTHIANS 12:4–6

In the stillness, your heart whispers secrets of the Divine, who gifts you with a gentle, flowing river of grace. Here, amid the hush of God's creation, your soul discerns the soft echoes of his voice. Each word, a gift bestowed, illuminates your path with celestial light, guiding you toward your God-given purpose.

In the quiet, where thoughts settle to a serene murmur, you find yourself in the presence of the Almighty's tender gaze. It is in this quiet calm that the Spirit's gifts, diverse and abundant, are revealed. Each unique blessing blends into the masterpiece of his grander plan.

In the sacred, the ordinary becomes a hallowed ground for spiritual encounters. Here the Spirit's gifts flourish. As you obtain tranquility, you grow attuned to the rhythm of divine grace, which nurtures your gifts to bloom in the eternal love of the Father, Son, and Holy Spirit.

GUIDED MEDITATION

Focused Scriptural Meditation

Ponder 1 Corinthians 12:4–6 and recognize the unique gifts the Spirit bestows upon you.

Reflective Prayer and Listening

Bare your soul now to seek an understanding of your spiritual gifts. Ask God to reveal how each serves his purpose.

Contemplation and Gratitude

In gratitude, accept your God-given gifts. Contemplate using them in God's service.

IMAGINATIVE CONTEMPLATION

Imagine a humble room where a gathering of faithful souls stands with you, each unique yet united in sacred purpose. Your hands, trembling slightly, accept a humble offering, a divine gift. You feel the weight of the gift not as a burden but as a glorious unfolding of divine intent.

Each soul in the room is anointed with gifts as varied as the stars. There is one who speaks in tongues you don't know, another whose hands bring healing, and a third who prophesies with the clarity of ancient seers. Yet your gift gleams with no less brilliance. In this sacred communion, you understand that each gift is vital to the Lord's design. Your gift, small as it may seem, is crucial for the harmony of God's kingdom. Welcome it, for in this gift lies your pathway to a deeper communion with the Divine.

ECHOED VERSES

Hold (hands over heart):

Heavenly Father, your gifts are as vast as your love.

Receive (hands open):

I open my heart to your spiritual endowments.

Hold (hands over heart):

Lord Christ, I find my true purpose in your service.

Receive (hands open):

Empower me to serve with grace and strength.

Hold (hands over heart):

Holy Spirit, you unify our diverse talents.

Receive (hands open):

May I use my gifts to glorify you.

SOULFUL BREATHING

Inhale deeply and whisper, *I receive the Spirit's gifts.* Breathe in unity and diversity, feeling the empowering presence of God in every breath.

Exhale slowly, whispering, *Variety of service to the Lord.* Understand with each release that there is a variety of service but only one Lord. Let go of burdens, feel the oneness of God's activities, and calm your soul with each breath.

Inhale: *I receive the Spirit's gifts.*

Exhale: *Variety of service to the Lord.*

Rest in stillness now. Let these words dwell within: *God empowers all.* Feel his peace and understand your unity with other believers in him, that we are connected deeply through his wondrous, diverse blessings. Conclude this exercise by recalling how there are different spiritual gifts and types of service but how they all come from the same source: the Holy Spirit.

SOULFUL REFLECTIONS

How do you perceive the unique gifts the Holy Spirit has granted to you, and how might you harness these gifts to serve God's purpose?

Reflect on how you can transform your daily activities into acts of service to the Lord. In what areas can you embody his love in your life?

CLOSING BENEDICTION

In the grace of our Lord Jesus Christ, may you, beloved in faith, be enriched with the diverse gifts bestowed on you by the same Spirit who blesses all believers. Even though the Spirit manifests in varied forms of service, may your life be a testament to the unity and love of our one Lord. In your journey, may the one true God guide and empower your activities, illuminating the path he has set. May your gifts serve as a reflection of his divine purpose. In exercising your gifts, may you always remember the source of your strength and the unity of the Spirit in the bond of peace. Let each day be an opportunity to glorify God through your unique contributions as you rejoice in the fellowship of the Holy Spirit. Go forth in peace and love, serving the Lord with gladness and humility in the name of Jesus. Amen.

Kingdom

Prioritizing God's Will

"Seek first the kingdom of God and his righteousness,
and all these things will be added to you."
MATTHEW 6:33

In the stillness, you find a peaceful sanctuary where whispers of God's will resonate, echoing in the chambers of heart. Here, beneath the star-studded blanket of his creation, your soul learns to listen. The world's chaos fades in this holy tranquility, and his voice, gentle yet potent, beckons you closer.

In the quiet, you unearth the treasure you find when you give God priority in your life. Each breath becomes a prayer, an intimate dialogue with your Creator. The rush of life slows to a sacred crawl, aligning your steps with his. Today's verse unveils its depth in this serene solitude, guiding you to seek his kingdom and righteousness first. Everything else will come in his time, his will, and his way.

In the sacred truth of Matthew 6:33, priorities shift, and worldly desires diminish in the glow of his eternal promise. You can find clarity and peace as you look at your to-do list and decide which tasks most honor God. Here your journey becomes a testament to faith, a dance of devotion, as you receive the peace found only in pursuing and prioritizing the will of the Father, Son, and Holy Spirit.

GUIDED MEDITATION

Focused Scriptural Meditation

As you consider Matthew 6:33, let God's promise to add all you need resonate within you.

Reflective Prayer and Listening

In sacred connection, speak to God about your desires and challenges. Listen for his guidance. Trust his provision.

Contemplation and Gratitude

Reflect on God's faithfulness. Offer gratitude for his unwavering presence and assurance.

IMAGINATIVE CONTEMPLATION

Imagine yourself in a serene meadow under a sky painted with the soft hues of dawn. Before you, a narrow path winds through the heart of the meadow. It's a journey toward something more splendid, a pursuit of a kingdom not of this earth. The path is your quest for the Divine and your yearning for his righteousness.

In this sacred space, the burdens of worldly cares lighten as if lifted by unseen hands. Here, in the presence of the Creator, your heart aligns with his will. Your soul, nourished by his Word, blooms like the wildflowers of the meadow. This moment, fleeting yet eternal, reminds you of a pervasive truth: as you seek his kingdom first, your Father will lovingly bestow upon you all else that you need, all that your heart truly desires.

ECHOED VERSES

Hold (hands over heart):

Heavenly Father, you guide me in paths of righteousness.

Receive (hands open):

Open my heart to follow your lead.

Hold (hands over heart):

Lord Christ, you light my way in darkness.

Receive (hands open):

Teach me to walk in your truth.

Hold (hands over heart):

Holy Spirit, you gently whisper wisdom.

Receive (hands open):

Help me hear and receive your guidance.

SOULFUL BREATHING

Breathe in deeply. *I seek first the kingdom of God.* Let his righteousness fill your lungs. With each breath, absorb his promise, feeling his divine assurance and eternal love. Now hold that breath for a moment as you absorb the guarantee of his care.

Exhale slowly, releasing doubts as you whisper, *And all these things shall follow.* Let go of worldly concerns, breathe out anxieties, and know the tranquility of his righteous path.

Inhale: *I seek first the kingdom of God.*

Exhale: *And all these things shall follow.*

Continue this cadence, allowing each breath to remind you to seek, aim at, and strive for his kingdom and righteousness. In stillness, let God's Word resonate: his kingdom is your priority; his righteousness your path. Feel his peace within, a calm assurance of his providential care and everlasting love.

SOULFUL REFLECTIONS

How does your daily life reflect a pursuit of God's kingdom and righteousness, and in what ways can you deepen your commitment to align your actions and choices with his will?

In seeking God's kingdom first, how do you balance your desires and needs with his divine plan, and what steps can you take to trust more fully in his provision and guidance?

CLOSING BENEDICTION

May the grace of our Lord Jesus Christ enfold you as you seek first the kingdom of God and his righteousness. In your daily journey, may you tune your heart to the whisper of his Spirit and allow him to guide you in paths of truth and love. As you prioritize his will above all else, may he meet your needs with his abundant provision. In every moment of uncertainty, may his Word be your steadfast light, and in times of abundance, may gratitude fill your heart. May the peace of God, which surpasses all understanding, guard your heart and mind in Christ Jesus. As you walk in obedience, let your life testify to his faithfulness and love. In the name of Jesus, go forth with courage and hope, for your heavenly Father watches over you. Amen.

DAY 39

Anticipate

Waiting for God's Timing

Faith is the assurance of things hoped for,
the conviction of things not seen.
HEBREWS 11:1

In the stillness, you find a sacred whisper, a gentle nudge of the soul. Like a delicate dawn breaking the night, unyielding faith arises within you. Hope becomes tangible, a lighted silhouette against the darkness, shaping your anticipation of God's perfect timing.

In the quiet, your heart listens for the rhythm of divine promises, which pulses like a beacon in the fog. Each beat reminds you of things you hope for, and each silence is a space for things you do not see. Here, in the hush of God's presence, your faith weaves a fabric of trust, intertwining the seen with the concealed, the known with the mysterious.

In the sacred pause, you stand at the threshold of eternity, where time bows to the Almighty. This holy moment cradles your soul, teaching you to patiently await the unseen workings of the Creator. Here faith transforms from concept to companion, guiding you on an invisible journey and illuminating the path of hope with the gentle light of the Father, Son, and Holy Spirit.

GUIDED MEDITATION

Focused Scriptural Meditation

Reflect on Hebrews 11:1 and on how faith is your assurance of what you hope for, your conviction of what you do not see.

Reflective Prayer and Listening

In heartfelt supplication, express your anticipation of God's timing. Share your hopes and unseen dreams with him.

Contemplation and Gratitude

In silent gratitude, thank God for the gift of faith. Cherish the peace that comes from his unseen work in your life.

IMAGINATIVE CONTEMPLATION

In the quiet of dawn, you stand at the edge of a vast, misty valley. As you gaze over the landscape, your heart is heavy with hopes not yet fulfilled, dreams still taking shape. Yet in this sacred moment, a gentle whisper of faith stirs within you. You feel the assurance of things hoped for, the conviction of unseen promises.

The sun rises higher, and the fog slowly lifts, revealing the lush green expanse below. There you see a vision of what awaits in God's perfect timing, things unseen yet ever certain. It's a reminder that beauty and growth are in the anticipation and the waiting. This is the essence of faith, a trust beyond sight, a belief in what has yet to manifest.

ECHOED VERSES

Hold (hands over heart):

Heavenly Father, you are my strength; I wait in faith.

Receive (hands open):

In stillness, I receive your peace, which surpasses understanding.

Hold (hands over heart):

Lord Christ, your promises are true; I trust your timing.

Receive (hands open):

Grace flows as I live out your perfect plan, Lord.

Hold (hands over heart):

Holy Spirit, guide me; your path is my desire.

Receive (hands open):

With open hands, heart ready, I welcome your divine guidance.

SOULFUL BREATHING

Inhale deeply, embracing faith's assurance, the certainty of blessings hoped for. Whisper, *Faith is assurance and hope.* Let each inhale fill you with conviction, mirroring the depth of omnipotent truth found in Hebrews. Breathe in hope.

Exhale slowly, releasing doubts and feeling the surety of unseen things. Whisper, *Conviction in unseen strength.* As you breathe out, let go of uncertainty, embody the conviction of today's verse, and find serenity in God's promises.

Inhale: *Faith is assurance and hope.*

Exhale: *Conviction in unseen strength.*

Rest in stillness, letting God's Word resonate in your heart. Obtain his peace, feeling faith's assurance and conviction's strength. In this quiet, discover a deeper connection with God's timeless truth.

SOULFUL REFLECTIONS

In moments of uncertainty, how do you see your faith reflecting the assurance of things hoped for and the conviction of things not seen?

As you journey through life's trials and tribulations, how do you perceive God's unseen hand guiding your path and shaping your character to align with his purpose and will for you?

CLOSING BENEDICTION

In the gracious love of Jesus Christ, may your heart find the patience to wait on the Lord. In times of anticipation, when the path seems veiled in the shadow of the unknown, may your faith stand firm, a testament to God's unseen yet ever-present hand. Remember, beloved, that his timing surpasses all understanding; he crafts moments and opportunities in perfect alignment with his will. May the assurance of things hoped for and the conviction of things not seen, as declared in Hebrews 11, clothe your spirit. Let your steps be guided not by sight but by the penetrating trust in his divine plan. May his peace, which transcends all understanding, guard your heart and mind in Christ Jesus. And in the waiting, may you discover the depth of his unfailing love and the strength of your unwavering faith. Amen.

Renewal

Embracing Renewed Faith

They who wait for the LORD shall renew their strength;
they shall mount up with wings like eagles;
they shall run and not be weary;
they shall walk and not faint.

ISAIAH 40:31

In the stillness, your heart whispers a sacred truth, sighing like a gentle breeze. Here, beneath the hush of earthly clamor, you find a haven for weary thoughts. This holy, divine presence cradles you, renewing your strength and lifting your burdens.

In the quiet, there lies a compelling promise as ancient as the stars yet as fresh as the morning dew. In these silent moments, your spirit, unburdened of the cacophony of life, listens intently. God's presence is a soothing balm, restoring and rejuvenating your innermost being.

In the sacred pause of life, when time seems to stand still, your soul stretches its wings like an eagle soaring high above the world's disorder; you rise, borne aloft on the winds of the Lord's unfailing love. Here you discover the power to walk unfaltering, to run undeterred toward the Father, Son, and Holy Spirit.

GUIDED MEDITATION

Focused Scriptural Meditation

Contemplate Isaiah 40:31 as you envision the strength the Lord gives to those who wait on him.

Reflective Prayer and Listening

In spiritual reflection, express your trust in God's will. Feel your strength renewed and your spirit uplifted.

Contemplation and Gratitude

Reflect on this renewal. Offer gratitude for the Father's endless support and rejuvenating power in your life.

IMAGINATIVE CONTEMPLATION

In the stillness of your heart, you find yourself standing on a vast plain. The golden sunrise stretches boundlessly above. Gazing skyward, you behold eagles soaring, their wings majestic against the heavens. You feel a stirring within, a call to rise above the mundane and know the freedom the eagles embody. As these noble birds glide without effort, you sense your spirit lifting to soar over worry and doubt.

Feel now the wind's gentle caress whispering God's promises. Each breath you take renews your strength, invigorating your being. You are running yet not weary; you are walking yet not faint. In this sacred moment, you are one with the Creator, understanding the boundless love and strength he bestows. You stand renewed, ready to journey forth with faith as your wings and his Word as your path.

ECHOED VERSES

Hold (hands over heart):

Heavenly Father, you promise strength to the weary.

Receive (hands open):

I open my heart to your power.

Hold (hands over heart):

Lord Christ, in you I find unwavering hope.

Receive (hands open):

Your love renews my spirit daily.

Hold (hands over heart):

Holy Spirit, guide my steps always.

Receive (hands open):

Embracing your light, I walk forward.

SOULFUL BREATHING

Inhale deeply, whispering, *Wait for the Lord.* Feel your spirit lift like soaring eagles and envision strength renewing you. Each breath brings God's promises closer, elevating your soul in tranquil faith.

Exhale slowly, releasing your prayer: *Renew my strength.* Feel weariness dissolve, replaced by divine energy. With every breath out, surrender doubts; receive his enduring presence, which calms your soul and empowers your journey.

Inhale: *Wait for the Lord.*

Exhale: *Renew my strength.*

Rest in this stillness and peace. Let these words dwell in your heart: his strength is yours. In his presence, find unyielding peace and an ever-renewing connection with God. As you breathe and wait for the Lord, expecting him, looking for him, and placing your hope in him, you will experience a remarkable transformation. Your strength will be renewed.

SOULFUL REFLECTIONS

How has waiting on the Lord transformed your understanding of patience and faith? How has it guided you toward a deeper trust in his timing and plans for your life?

In moments of weariness or doubt, how do you find strength in God's promises? How do you allow his Word to uplift and sustain you as you journey closer to his heart?

CLOSING BENEDICTION

Blessed child of the Most High, may the Lord guide your steps on his path of righteousness. As you walk in the light of his Word, may your faith be renewed like the eagle's soaring strength. In your moments of waiting, find solace in his unchanging grace, for the Lord shall reward your patience with unfailing strength. May your heart be steadfast, anchored in the eternal love of your Savior. In every trial, may you feel the comforting presence of the Holy Spirit guiding you to run and not grow weary, to walk and not faint. In your journey, may you embody the love and mercy that your heavenly Father bestows upon you. In the name of Jesus, go forth with a spirit rejuvenated by his promise, carrying his light into every corner of your life. Amen.

ACKNOWLEDGMENTS

As I reflect on the journey of creating this book, my heart overflows with gratitude for the many individuals who have played a crucial role in bringing this work to life. First and foremost, I want to express my deepest appreciation to my beloved wife, Laurie, who has been my unwavering rock throughout this process. Your constant love, support, and encouragement have been the driving force behind my ability to pour my heart and soul into these pages. I am forever grateful for your presence in my life.

To our incredible children, Wesley, Brad, and Jessica. Thank you for being my pillars of strength and always believing in me. Your love and support have been a constant source of inspiration, pushing me to strive for excellence in everything I do. I am blessed to have you as my family, and I am proud of the fantastic individuals you have become.

I extend my heartfelt thanks to the countless friends who have stood by my side, offering encouragement and emotional support when I needed it most. Your friendship has been a true gift, and I am grateful for the laughter, the tears, and the countless memories we have shared.

To Tim, Jessica, and Caroline, the incredible editors and proofreaders at BroadStreet Publishing. I am indebted to you for your tireless efforts in refining this manuscript. Your keen eyes, insightful feedback, and dedication to excellence have elevated this book to new heights. Thank you for your patience, expertise, and unwavering commitment to bringing out the best in my work.

I also want to express my gratitude to Whitney Gossett and her remarkable team at Content Capital. Your guidance, support, and expertise have been instrumental in bringing this book to fruition. Thank you for believing in my vision and working tirelessly to ensure that this message reaches the hearts and minds of readers worldwide.

To the *EncounterPodcast* family worldwide, your unwavering support and encouragement humble me. Your prayers, kind words, and financial contributions have been a true blessing, enabling me to dedicate myself fully to the research and writing of this book. I am forever grateful for your generosity and for the impact you have had on my life.

Finally, to my precious grandchildren, the light of my life. I want to thank you for the joy and love you bring into my world daily. Being your grandfather is one of my most cherished honors, and I am grateful for the opportunity to share my wisdom and experiences with you. This book is a testament to the power of faith, love, and the unbreakable bond of family.

With love and gratitude,

Drew

ABOUT THE AUTHOR

Dr. Drew Dickens is a visionary leader and scholar who has significantly contributed to the intersection of technology, spirituality, and faith-based engagement. He holds a doctorate in liberal studies and theological anthropology from Southern Methodist University, where his groundbreaking dissertation explored the impact of generative AI on spiritual direction, positioning him as a thought leader in this emerging field.

As the founder of the Encountering Peace: Meditation app and *EncounterPodcast*, Drew has created a thriving community of over three hundred thousand daily subscribers seeking to deepen their spiritual lives and encounter God amid the chaos of life. Previously, he served as the director of content for the Abide meditation app and established Need Him Global, a ministry that leverages cutting-edge media to engage people from diverse backgrounds in meaningful conversations about faith.

With a master's from Dallas Theological Seminary and Baylor University, Drew brings a depth of theological knowledge and academic rigor to his innovative approaches to spirituality and faith-based engagement. His unique perspective and expertise have made him a sought-after speaker, consultant, and collaborator in the fields of ministry, technology, and personal growth. Through his multifaceted work, Drew continues to push the boundaries of what is possible at the intersection of faith and technology, inspiring others to embrace new ways of connecting with the Divine and cultivating a more profound sense of purpose and meaning in their lives.